Preface books

A series of scholarly and critical studies of major writers intended for those needing modern and authoritative guidance through the characteristic difficulties of their work to reach an intelligent understanding and enjoyment of it.

General Editor: MAURICE HUSSEY

Available now:

A Preface to Wordsworth	JOHN PURKIS
A Preface to Donne	JAMES WINNY
A Preface to Milton	LOIS POTTER
A Preface to Coleridge	ALLAN GRANT
A Preface to Jane Austen	CHRISTOPHER GILLIE
A Preface to Yeats	EDWARD MALINS
A Preface to Pope	I.R.F. GORDON
A Preface to Hardy	MERRYN WILLIAMS
A Preface to Dryden	DAVID WYKES

Other titles in preparation:

A Preface to Spenser	HELENA SHIRE
A Preface to Dickens	ALLAN GRANT

A Preface to Milton

Lois Potter

Longman

LONGMAN GROUP LIMITED
London

*Associated companies, branches and
representatives throughout the world*

© Longman Group Ltd 1971

First published 1971
Second impression 1978

ISBN 0 582 31508 5 Paper

*Printed in Hong Kong by
Sing Cheong Printing Co Ltd*

Contents

List of Illustrations

Acknowledgements

Milton's poems are quoted in the text of the edition by John Carey and Alastair Fowler (*The Poems of John Milton*, Longman, 1968).

I should like to thank Dr T. E. Hartley, Dr A. J. Meadows, Mr P. G. Scott and Dr J. R. Watson for their advice and encouragement.

The author and publisher are grateful to the following for permission to reproduce photographs: S. K. Agarwala, page 33; Lord Barnard and the Courtauld Institute of Art, page 161; Bibliothèque Nationale, page 19; British Museum, pages 28, 47 and 90–1; Earl of Cawdor, page 93; Devonshire Collection, Chatsworth: Reproduced by permission of the Trustees of the Chatsworth Settlement, photo from the Courtauld Institute of Art, page 96; N. Hancock, page 25; Mansell Collection, pages 16 and 134; National Portrait Gallery, pages 8, 160 *left* and *right;* Radio Times Hulton Picture Library, *frontispiece;* Trinity College, Cambridge, page 110; University Library, Cambridge, pages 14, 41, 63, 139 and 175.

The painting of the Garden of Eden by P. P. Rubens and J. Brueghel reproduced on the cover is by courtesy of the Mauritshuis, the Hague and is reversed from the original.

DR LOIS POTTER, who took her doctorate at Girton College, Cambridge, is now teaching English in the University of Leicester. This is her first book.

To my Mother and Father

Foreword

The image of Milton that will be derived from this book is, so to speak, that of the portrait of p. 8 rather than the hardened embittered one of the frontispiece: a Puritan but, first of all, a sensitive and studious humanist committed to intellectual freedom and to the didactic and aesthetic virtues of the arts. Admittedly, any approach to poetry through contemporaneous work in other fields of art may have its dangers but it evidently succeeds with a growing number of readers. It is remarkable that a man most familiar as a blind writer who had to use subtly evasive action in places like the description of Eden in *Paradise Lost* Book IV and concentrate on the smells, tastes and sounds* should be able to recapture the visual aspect of the Baroque. This is one of Lois Potter's principal themes.

In the seventeenth century all learning was supported by a diversity of classical, mythological and medieval opinions, yet at the same time it was increasingly and tentatively subjected to the impact of more modern scientific discoveries. Where Oxford fostered the less austere courtier and monarchist, Cambridge was the mecca of the Puritan and the philosopher of science. The swelling of these currents meant that Milton was the last major English poet to avail himself of the philosophy that informed Chaucer and, to a lesser extent, Shakespeare. Imaginatively, as we see on p. 43, he kept the options open and placed the Ptolemaic, Copernican and Galilean world models side by side, unwilling to cut himself off from the early world whose mythology he interpreted with such depth and understanding.

Dr Potter has selected a number of themes from a wealth of scholarship; she provides the intellectual core for the student and then demonstrates how it may be placed at the disposal of the poetry, not forgetting the 'Milton sound' which prefers his verse to be read aloud. Miltonic scholarship of an older generation insisted that a lifetime of Greek and Latin grammar alone could equip one with the necessary expertise for reading Milton. *A Preface to Milton* shows that the demands are much more attractive and variegated and that the poetry is well within the grasp of a modern sensibility.

General Editor MAURICE HUSSEY

*Consider the imagery here:

> Groves whose rich trees wept odorous gums and balm,
> Others whose fruit burnished with golden rind
> Hung amiable, Hesperian fables true,
> If true, here only, and of delicious taste:
> (*PL* IV. 247–51)

1 Biographical summaries

Chronological table

1603–25		Reign of James I.
1608	John Milton born, 9 December, at the sign of the Spread Eagle, Bread Street, London.	
1620–25	Attends St Paul's School, London.	
1625–49		Reign of Charles I.
1625	Admitted to Christ's College, Cambridge.	
1629	Graduates B.A., 26 March. *Ode on the Morning of Christ's* Nativity, 25 December. Portrait (p. 8) painted.	Charles I dissolves Parliament and attempts to govern alone.
1629–32	Continues studies for M.A., which he receives 3 July 1632. *The Passion* (unfinished), Italian sonnets, *Arcades, On Time, At a Solemn Musick*, epitaph on Shakespeare, and *L'Allegro* and *Il Penseroso* probably belong to this period.	
1632–35	Begins ambitious reading programme in Hammersmith, living with his parents. Sonnet: *'How soon hath time'*.	
1633		Laud Archbishop of Canterbury.
1634	*Comus* performed at Ludlow Castle, 29 September.	

1635–38	Milton continues reading programme at Horton, Bucks.	
1637	Death of Milton's mother. *Comus* published.	Controversy over Ship Money. Charles I orders Scots to accept English Prayer Book.
1638	*Lycidas* published in a collection of poems, *Justa Eduardo King.*	Scottish 'Solemn League and Covenant'.
1638–39	Milton travels in France, Italy, and Switzerland.	
1639	Returned to London, he becomes teacher to, along others, his nephews, John and Edward Phillips.	First Bishops' War.
1640	Publishes *Epitaphium Damonis*, a Latin elegy on his friend Diodati.	Short Parliament, 13 April–5 May. Second Bishops' War. Long Parliament begins session, 3 November, and arrests Strafford and Laud.
1641	Begins writing pamphlets on Church government, advocating abolition of the bishops.	Strafford executed. Parliament debates Root and Branch Petition for abolition of episcopacy and Grand Remonstrance (indictment of royal policy) narrowly passes Commons.
1642	Marries Mary Powell, probably in early summer. In July or August she returns to her parents in Oxfordshire.	Civil War begins, 22 August. Battle of Edgehill, 23 October. Royalist army headquarters in Oxford. Turnham Green, November.
1643	Milton publishes *Doctrine and Discipline of Divorce* (followed by other divorce pamphlets in 1644 and 1645).	Parliament forms alliance with Scotland and takes Covenant.

1644	*Of Education* and *Areopagitica.*	Battle of Marston Moor, 2 July.
1645	Milton is reunited with his wife.	Laud executed, January. Battle of Naseby, 14 June.
1646	Publication of his poems, 2 January (title page gives year as 1645). First daughter, Anne, born, 29 July.	King takes refuge with Scots. Oxford surrenders.
1647	Deaths of Milton's father, and father-in-law, Richard Powell.	King a prisoner, first of Scots, then of army.
1648	Second daughter, Mary, born 25 October.	Army enters London, with King its prisoner. 'Pride's Purge' of Parliament leaves only extremists, known as the Rump.
1649	*On the Tenure of Kings and Magistrates.* Milton, appointed Secretary for the Foreign Tongues to the Council of State, answers *Eikon Basilike* (supposedly written by King) with *Eikonoklastes.*	Execution of Charles I, 30 January. Commonwealth proclaimed.
1650		Charles II goes to Scotland and wins Presbyterian support by taking the Covenant. Cromwell defeats Scottish army at Dunbar, 3 September.
1651	*Pro Populo Anglicano Defensio (A Defence of the English People)* published to vindicate the Commonwealth abroad. Son, John, born 16 March.	Final defeat of Charles II's army at Battle of Worcester, 3 September.

1652	Milton totally blind by this year. Birth of daughter, Deborah, 2 May. Death of Mary Powell, 5 May, and her son in June. *Samson Agonistes* may have been begun at this time.	
1653		Cromwell dissolves Rump and begins Protectorate.
1654	*Defensio Secunda* continues the international debate on the Commonwealth's actions.	
1655	*Defensio pro Se*. Most of Milton's English sonnets probably written by this time.	Piedmont massacre.
1656	Milton marries Katherine Woodcock. Begins *Christian Doctrine*.	
1657	Birth of daughter, Katherine, 19 October.	Second Protectorate.
1658	Milton's wife and baby daughter die. He probably begins writing *Paradise Lost* about this time.	Death of Cromwell, 3 September.
1659	*Treatise of Civil Power; Means to Remove Hirelings from the Church*.	Abdication of Richard Cromwell and restoration of government by the Rump.
1660	*A Ready and Easy Way to Establish A Free Commonwealth*. After Restoration, Milton is briefly imprisoned but set free and given royal pardon.	Restoration of Charles II, 30 May. Punishment of regicides.
1663	Marries Elizabeth Minshull.	

1665	Lives briefly in Chalfont St Giles because of plague, and shows a friend the MS of *Paradise Lost.*	The Great Plague of London.
1666		The Great Fire of London.
1667	Publication of *Paradise Lost* (in ten books).	
1670	*History of Britain* published.	
1671	*Paradise Regained and Samson Agonistes* published together.	
1673	*Of True Religion.* New edition of *Poems.*	
1674	Second edition of *Paradise Lost,* now in twelve books. Milton died of gout, probably on 8 November, and was buried on the 12th in St Giles, Cripplegate.	

Education and reading

In his pamphlet *Of Education*, Milton defines 'a complete and generous education' as being 'that which fits a man to perform justly, skilfully, and magnanimously all the offices, both private and public, of peace and war'. He was not altogether satisfied that his own education had fulfilled this goal; nevertheless it was the best that money could buy in the seventeenth century, and he never ceased to be grateful to his father for making it possible.

The environment in which he grew up was one of strong and somewhat radical piety combined with respect for learning and the arts. There was a tradition of religious stubbornness: his grandfather had suffered for his Catholicism in the reign of Elizabeth I, while his father, a gifted musician and composer, was disinherited by the old man for turning Protestant, and took up the profession of scrivener (a combination of notary, clerk, and money lender). The parish priest, Richard Stock, was a Puritan, and Thomas Young, Milton's first tutor, was a Scottish Presbyterian. Milton's family was musical as well as religious. He learned to play the organ and sing, and later on he taught singing to others. From the many references to music in his poetry, it is clear that he had rather more than the bare minimum of knowledge which every gentleman was supposed to acquire.

When Thomas Young left to take up a post in one of the non-conformist communities on the continent, Milton was sent to St Paul's School. It was a place well suited to enhance both his piety and his sense of his own importance: the boys were urged to model themselves on the Child Jesus, to whom the school was dedicated. Here Milton made some of his closest friends, particularly Charles Diodati, began to compose poetry in English, Latin, and Greek, and, reading at late hours in his enthusiasm for study, paved the way for his eventual blindness.

The typical Latin grammar school curriculum of the period involved a thorough knowledge of the major Latin and Greek writers (St Paul's offered more Greek than most), with special emphasis on Virgil, whom the students had to know almost by heart. Not only did they discuss the texts in detail, analysing grammatical and rhetorical devices and following up geographical and mythological allusions, they were also expected to assimilate and imitate the style of the best models. As a first step, they experimented with the word order of a few lines of Ovid or Virgil; later they might take an English translation and try to turn it back into something as close as possible to the original Latin. When they finally began composing poems of their own, the result was bound to be derivative, but that was the intention. Schoolmasters hoped that writing in the beautiful cadences of the *Aeneid* would become second nature to their students, and that the half-conscious echoes of earlier works would produce a poetry rich in literary allusions. At the same time, the St Paul's curriculum included many references to contemporary literature. The headmaster, Alexander Gill, frequently used examples from Spenser, Sidney and Daniel to illustrate features of English grammar, and his son Alexander, another friend of Milton's, was himself a poet.

Compared with this lively metropolitan school, Cambridge, which Milton entered at the usual age of sixteen, seemed to him a provincial backwater. He probably chose to go there rather than to Oxford because in the Elizabethan and early Jacobean period Cambridge had had a number of famous Puritan preachers and a strong tradition of Puritanism, particularly in Emmanuel, Sidney Sussex, and Milton's own college, Christ's. By 1625 most of the great preachers were either dead or retired. Milton's main objections to Cambridge, however, were not so much those of a Puritan as of a scholar who felt that he was not being helped to learn anything worth while. As he saw it, those students who really wanted to work were held back by an outmoded educational system, while the others simply did not bother to work at all. Moreover, he had trouble getting on with his tutor. Exactly what happened is not clear, but it looks as if Milton was actually rusticated early in his second year, though he seems

not to have felt himself in disgrace (he said later that he left the university without any stain on his character). At any rate, he returned to Cambridge in the following term and was assigned another tutor, with whom his relations seem to have been satisfactory.

Law, medicine and divinity were the three professions for which the university prepared students, and of these divinity was the most popular. Milton, who planned to enter the Church, could look forward to about twenty years of study before he would earn the degree of Doctor of Divinity. The first part of the university course consisted of logic, rhetoric, arithmetic and music; later, the student moved on to philosophy. Teaching was done by means of lectures—mostly in Latin, but with a few in English—and public disputations, in which every student, after his second year, was expected to take his turn. There were no written examinations, but these debates supplied a means of assessing students, and a candidate for the B.A. degree was expected to defend an argument against all contenders. Whether he believed in it or not did not matter; in any case, many of the debates were on such uninspiring subjects as 'Partial forms do not occur in an animal in addition to the whole'.

Milton later published some of his contributions to these academic exercises, at which he seems to have been an impressive performer, despite his conviction that they were a waste of time, a distraction from his private studies. When he found the assigned topic boring he said so, but tried to make it as entertaining as possible for his listeners. On subjects that really interested him, such as a defence of learning or a discussion of the music of the spheres, he showed an ability to combine wide reading with high eloquence and, more surprisingly perhaps, with humour. It is true that Milton was never one for the light touch: all his life he was an inveterate punner and his jokes are heavy even when they are not sarcastic in tone, but this is often true of undergraduate humour. He frequently struck a personal note in his speeches—thus we learn, for example, that his relations with his fellow students improved over the years, though he had to put up with being nicknamed 'the Lady' because of his youthful appearance and dislike of coarse behaviour.

He was very sarcastic, at the expense of those who called him by this name, in one of the most interesting of his public speeches, the one delivered at a Vacation Exercise (traditionally a lighthearted celebration of the end of the academic year) in 1628. It seems rather odd that 'the Lady' should have been asked to be master of ceremonies on such a rowdy occasion, but he lived up to his role, producing a burlesque Latin speech so coarse that translators tend to leave parts of it in the original. Then, with a characteristic change of mood, he began to recite in English verse ('*Hail native language*'), and told his audience how much he would have preferred to be dealing with 'some graver subject'. After this brief lyrical digression he returned to the free and easy manner suitable for the occasion, but this is the first of many passages in his works which hint at high ambitions and the sense of a great destiny.

In all, Milton was at Cambridge for seven years. He was placed fourth out of 259 candidates for the Bachelor's degree in 1629, and received his M.A. *cum laude* in 1632. Despite his Puritan background he must still have regarded himself as a member of the Church of England, since his conscience did nòt prevent him from going through the formality of subscribing to its Articles in order to obtain his degree. He may have been offered a fellowship; if so, he turned it down. Instead, he decided to spend the next few years in intensive reading on his own, while living with his parents. It was quiet and secluded on his father's country estate, but at the same time near enough to London for him to make occasional visits, as he wrote later, 'either for the sake of purchasing books, or of learning somewhat new in mathematics or in music'.

He was now in something of the same position as Faustus at the beginning of Marlowe's play, having to decide among the three learned professions of medicine, law and divinity—and, like Faustus, he eventually rejected all three. His friend Diodati had taken up the study of medicine, apparently after deciding against divinity; he had friends who were studying law at the Inns of Court; and, of course, his father almost certainly expected him to enter the Church. Much of his reading during this period, as appears from the notes which he made, was devoted to the writings of the Church Fathers and to Latin, Greek and Hebrew works on the history of the Christian Church, from which he concluded that 'those purer times were no such as they are cried up' (*Of Reformation*). At the same time, he kept up his reading in modern languages, which he had probably begun at schòol. His favourite was Italian, partly because of Diodati's family background, and it was in his copy of a translation of one of the great Italian epics, Ariosto's *Orlando Furioso*, that he wrote a Latin couplet bidding farewell to any thought of a legal career.

From the sonnet which he wrote early on in this period of private study (*'How soon hath time'*), it would seem that he felt some uneasiness at taking so long to settle down to a profession; time was passing quickly, 'But my late spring no bud or blossom sheweth'. By the time Milton was in his late twenties, his father also may have begun to think, or even to say, that his brilliant pious son, whom he had, after all, been supporting all this time, was not making much of a return on the investment. Two published poems and a masque were very little to show for so many years of study. Milton wrote an eloquent defence of the divine nature of poetry in a Latin poem addressed to his father; poetry and music were sister arts, he pointed out, and perhaps one day his talents might make the old man immortal. He had no doubts as to where his true vocation lay.

Even so, there was no reason why he should not combine poetry with a career in the Church. Two of the greatest seventeenth century poets, Donne and Herbert, were also churchmen who, like Milton, put off taking orders for many years because they felt themselves unworthy. What finally decided Milton against divinity, or at least gave him a presentable reason for deciding against it, was the increasingly authoritarian and conformist character which the Church had been taking on since Laud became Archbishop of Canterbury in 1633. To take holy orders now, Milton felt, would require him to renounce any right to think for himself, becoming instead one of the 'blind mouths' (as he called the clergy in *Lycidas*) who submitted to being used as mere spokesmen for a state Church. Opposition to Laud was widespread and it was possible that the situation would change if he waited long enough. Meanwhile, he could still serve God outside the established Church, perhaps as a freelance writer.

In 1637 Milton's mother died and in the following year he made a trip to France and Italy. He links the two events in his later autobiographical account, though without explaining their connection. Perhaps he had felt obliged to stay home while she was in poor health; perhaps the trip was intended to take his mind off her death. Late in the spring of 1638 Milton set out, with one servant. His father, as usual, was paying.

The Italian journey

Since the time of the Reformation, Italy had been regarded by English Protestants with a mixture of admiration and horror. It had never altogether ceased to be a source of inspiration, particularly in literature and dress, but at the same time it was thought of as the home of Machiavelli, the Borgias, and, above all, the Pope. This was less true of Venice than of the other Italian city-states. For a while, in the early years of the seventeenth century, it had actually seemed possible that the Republic might break away from the Church of Rome; it was still comparatively free of papal control and its University of Padua was the only one in Italy open to Protestants. On the other hand Rome, even under the liberal seventeenth-century popes, was felt to be a dangerous place to visit. Protestants were always urged to avoid it during Holy Week, when a house-to-house check was made to see that everyone took communion. It was said that if a Protestant fell ill there no physician was allowed to attend him until the wretched patient had first been terrorized into conversion.

Milton, with his head full of the classical masterpieces, was not to be deterred by such stories. Many years later, in his *Second Defence of the English People*, he poured scorn on the popular image of Italy, assuring an antagonist that the country 'was not, as you think, a refuge or asylum for criminals, but rather the lodging-place of *humanitas* and of all the arts of civilization'. He was well prepared

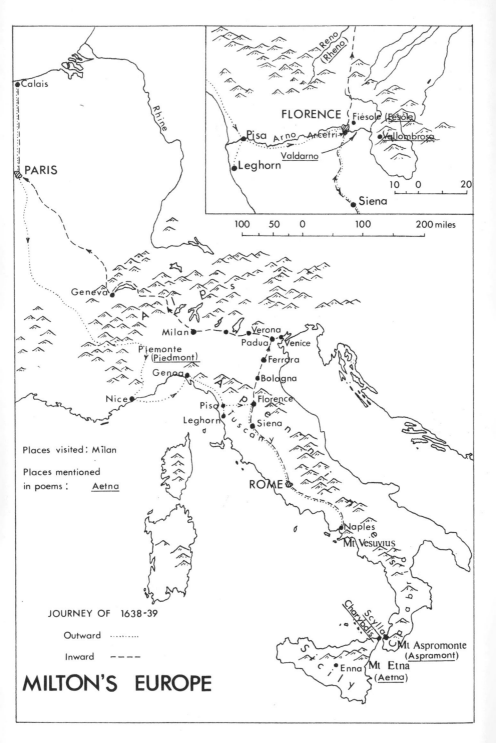

MILTON'S EUROPE

Places visited: Milan

Places mentioned
in poems : Aetna

JOURNEY OF 1638-39

Outward ....

Inward -----

for the journey, with his knowledge of Italian language and literature since Roman times. France, which he passed through on his way, held little interest for him; like many of his contemporaries, he thought of it as a lightheaded and frivolous place. Thus, after a short stay in Paris, he made his way as quickly as possible to the south.

He had originally planned a fairly extensive European tour. He was to have gone from southern Italy to Sicily (which had a special interest for him as the birthplace of pastoral poetry) and then to Greece. In the end, he got no further than Naples. Here, early in 1639, the news from England caught up with him. He learned that his closest friend, Charles Diodati, had died, and that Charles I was about to send troops into Scotland to enforce religious conformity there. As he said later, he felt it his duty to be in England at such a critical time; perhaps, also, his friend's death made him lose heart for further travel. He decided to return the way he had come, revisiting Rome and Florence and stopping also at Geneva, where Diodati's uncle was Professor of Divinity. In all, he was out of England for about a year and three months, and it was probably the happiest period of his life.

When he writes about his travels, it is of his new acquaintances in Italy that Milton has most to say; he did not regard himself as a sightseer, but rather as an ambassador from one culture to another. He was more fortunate than the typical modern traveller, since Latin was still an international language, though the Italians pronounced it differently (and, he came to think, better) than the English. He was also able to astonish his hosts with his fluency in their own language and the technical skill of the poems which he had composed in it. Thus, thanks to his own talents and to letters of introduction from the right people (such as Sir Henry Wotton, ex-ambassador to Venice, who had read and admired *Comus*), Milton found himself invited into the homes of the most distinguished Italian authors and patrons of art.

In particular, he was privileged to attend meetings of the famous Academies—literary and philosophical societies under noble patronage, which met, often in palatial surroundings, to hear scholarly papers and literary compositions. Their members included some of the greatest aristocrats, but a democratic spirit prevailed, particularly in the Venetian Republic: it was the custom there for the group called the *Incogniti* to attend their meetings in masks, so that the humbler members would not feel intimidated by the presence of those more nobly born. At such gatherings as these, Milton read some of his Latin and Italian compositions and took part in urbanely philosophical discussions, winning general admiration for his youthful charm and modesty as well as his talent. He found here what he had missed at Cambridge—friends who shared his intelligence and interests.

They did not, of course, share his religious beliefs. In theory Milton was always strongly anti-Catholic, but in practice he made

The Solfatara a volcanic field near Vesuvius, which Milton may have visited (see PL, *I 227–37), from Sandys,* Relation of a Journey, *1615*

friends with many individual Catholics. Those from whom he received kindnesses included the Vatican librarian and Cardinal Barberini, one of Rome's greatest art patrons. He prefixed to the 1645 edition of his poems a number of tributes in Latin and Italian which had been paid him by such men as Manso, once the patron of the great poet·Tasso, and Carlo Dati, a Florentine patrician and member of the Della Crusca Academy. He was never directly bothered by religious persecution, though at one point he was warned not to revisit Rome on his way north from Naples, because the Jesuits were supposed to be plotting against him; he ignored the warning and nothing happened. It was his policy, throughout his journey, to avoid bringing up religious questions himself, but to answer truthfully if anyone asked his opinions.

There were times when these opinions caused minor difficulties, as is apparent from Manso's Latin epigram on Milton, hinting that his religion is the only thing less than perfect about him. We see from *Areopagitica* that his visit to the blind Galileo, virtually a prisoner in his villa at Arcetri near Florence, remained in his mind as a symbol of how the free use of human reason could be stifled by religious bigotry. Nevertheless, his longing for friendship was much stronger than his hostility towards Catholicism. He had copies of his Latin elegy on Diodati sent to his Italian friends in the hope that some of them would write to him, and in 1647 was delighted to receive a letter from Carlo Dati (three earlier ones had been lost *en route*). He replied eagerly, offering to send his Latin poems, but asking Dati's indulgence for some rather strong anti-papal expressions in some of them. Dati's friendly reply, which paid him the compliment of writing in Italian, looked forward to receiving the poems but added that those against his religion, even from a friend, could 'only be excused, not praised'. His last letter to Milton, and the last one which Milton got from Italy, dates from the end of 1648. It was probably in the hope of renewing this correspondence that he praised a number of his Italian friends by name in an autobiographical passage of his *Second Defence* (1654), which he knew would be widely read on the continent. But he probably succeeded only in embarrassing them. By writing on behalf of the regicide government he had cut himself off forever from the orthodox Catholics.

It is not hard to see why someone so eager for friendship and so haunted by love of the past as Milton should have said more about these things than about the great works of modern art and architecture which he must have seen all around him in Italy. Even so, it is surprising that he says nothing at all about the latter, for such sights must have been entirely new in his experience. Since the Reformation, religious paintings had been considered a form of idolatry in England; only recently, under Laud's influence, had churches begun to acquire paintings depicting episodes from the lives of Christ or the saints. The artists patronized by the Tudors had been Protestants from Germany or the Netherlands. Italian painting was only beginning to be known to a few wealthy collectors, the greatest of whom was Charles I himself. Perhaps these associations with Laud and Charles I kept Milton from responding to what he saw. Italian art of the Counter-Reformation (usually dated from the end of the Council of Trent in 1563) attempted to counteract the spread of Protestantism by accentuating the emotional and popular elements of Catholicism. There was a greater reliance on dramatic, even sensational effects, as in paintings of the deaths and martyrdoms of saints, while church architecture became an expression of the power and wealth of the Church Militant. Much of this would have been anathema to Milton, though at the same time he may have wondered whether a Protestant artist could learn from the Catholic humanists how to put his belief in human reason and his admiration for classical culture to the service of God.

It would be interesting to know whether Milton saw more than the outside of St Peter's, which an English Protestant would have regarded as the temple of Antichrist. He must have thought it outrageously proud and extravagant. Yet at the time of Milton's visit to Rome the great architect and sculptor Bernini had scarcely begun the fantastic decoration of the interior which was to make Michelangelo's Renaissance cathedral a triumph of the Baroque style. What he finally created for the focal point of the building—the

huge canopy and the lofty throne of St Peter surmounted by a 'glory' of angels and saints—could almost have been a model for Satan's

> Throne of Royal State, which far
> Outshone the wealth of Ormus and of Ind
> (*PL* II. 1–2).

It has, in fact, been suggested that Pandemonium, with its gilded roof, *is* St Peter's; it might, on the other hand, be the ancient Roman Pantheon. Either way, Milton would be comparing the finest construction of a false religion to the palace of the devils from whom all false religions, pagan or Catholic, were derived.

Though Baroque art is often thought of as the artistic expression of the spirit of the Counter-Reformation and political absolutism, there are many qualities in Milton's work which could be described as Baroque: the sheer vastness of his treatment of both time and space, his strong contrasts of light and dark, and the sense of movement and conflict in his characters. It is tempting to think that he might in spite of himself have absorbed something of his aesthetic sensibility from, for instance, the painted ceilings of Italian palaces, where clouds and flying angels give the illusion of infinite space stretching above the spectator's head, or from the sculptures of Bernini, which make stone seem to move before one's eyes. The Sistine chapel of Michelangelo could have shown him the beauty of power in action; his Adam, even at the moment when God is creating life in him, is full of energy waiting to be roused.

But it is always risky to draw analogies between one art form and another. The Baroque qualities in Milton's poetry were there before he ever saw Italy, and men with poor eyesight (James Joyce is a modern example) tend not to have a strong visual memory. Milton may have looked down on the visual arts which, unlike poetry and music, were not taught at university. Even the scenery of Italy seems to have made less impression on him than the descriptions of it which he read in travel books. It is significant that in *Paradise Lost* he should compare Hell to Mount Aetna, which he had not seen, rather than to Vesuvius, which he had.

What did interest him was Italian music. When he was in Venice he shipped home a chest, not of paintings and statues, but of books of music by contemporary composers, including Monteverdi who was living in Venice at the time as organist of St Mark's. No doubt some of these may have been bought with his father in mind, but the opera scores would have been of interest to both of them. Milton had already written words to be set to music and was interested in the relationship of the two arts. In fact, despite his love of music, he seems to have thought of it almost exclusively as a means of making poetry more effective. He urges the 'Sphere-borne harmonious sisters, voice, and verse', to 'Wed your divine sounds', and praises Henry Lawes for setting words so as to bring out their meaning and not distort their sound; what he really means is that he believes in the subordination of music to verse. In the Latin *Ad Patrem* he goes so far as to say that music without words is meaningless: it was not Orpheus's lute-playing but his song that won the inhabitants of the underworld to pity him.

It was out of the attempt to re-create Greek tragedy that opera had first been developed in Italy at the end of the sixteenth century. The names given to this new art form ('opera' did not come into use until much later) were 'fable in music', 'drama for music'. These show the desire of their creators to achieve the union of the arts which they believed had existed in the time of the ancient Greeks. Like the English masque, operas were produced with great sumptuousness; in fact, the English masque designer Inigo Jones had visited Italy and picked up many of his ideas there. They differed from masques, however, in the range of sources which they dramatized; masques were purely allegorical, but operas made use of biblical, historical and mythological themes. Monteverdi's *Orfeo* (1607) has a fine libretto which treats Milton's favourite myth as an expression of the power of art and the weakness of human passion. After Orpheus has lost Eurydice for the second time, as a result of his too-great eagerness to see her again, the Chorus points out the ironic contrast between his victory over hell and his defeat by his own desires: 'Only he who wins over himself is worthy of eternal glory.' But there is a final apotheosis for Orpheus, who ascends with Apollo to heaven; earthly happiness is not for the great artist but he has his reward nevertheless. Milton, who had so recently been exploring these themes in *Lycidas*, must have been struck by the high seriousness of this work. In operas with a more overtly religious subject, the fusion of several arts in one which is characteristic of Baroque style was used to serve the Counter-Reformation purpose of presenting religion with the greatest possible emotional impact. The possibility of achieving a similar effect in English was to occupy Milton's mind for some time after his Italian journey, and *Samson Agonistes*, even though its main inspiration was Greek tragedy, would probably have been different if Milton had not been acquainted with the new art form that was Italian opera.

But the most important result of the Italian journey was its effect on Milton's self-confidence. Before he left England, he was simply a man of nearly thirty who, instead of committing himself to a profession, was still being financed in private study by his father. To set against this fact, he had only minor achievements: he had won some respect from his fellow-students and teachers at Cambridge, published a few verses anonymously, and written a masque which had finally to be published because manuscript copies were so much in demand. But to win praise outside his own country was another matter. The reception given to his Latin verses in the country of the Romans not only confirmed him in the conviction that his true profession was literature, it also, paradoxically, made him decide to write his masterpiece, whatever it might be, in English

Frontispiece of Andreini's tragedy L'Adamo, *1613, by Procaccino* 19

rather than the international tongue. There were two reasons for this. One was that the Italians themselves believed that the use and improvement of their own language was a sacred and patriotic duty, and Milton felt that he ought likewise to raise the dignity of the English language. Moreover, as he admitted later, he knew that it would be hard to reach even the second rank among the many great names who had already written in Latin. Italy had made him determined to settle for nothing less than immortality.

Political experience

Having returned to England in order to be part of its destiny at a crucial period, Milton at first seemed content simply to be a spectator. He took a house in the City and settled down to the life of a teacher, first tutoring his two nephews and then, probably, other pupils. This action was not so irrelevant to the times as it has seemed to some biographers. Along with a sense of his duty to his country, perhaps enhanced by the nationalism which he would have met abroad, it is not surprising if at last he accepted also the more mundane one of earning his own living. He recognized that his education was over, and that it was time for him to make use of what he had learned.

His political views were still unformed. The Laudian measures which led him to think of himself as having been 'Church-outed by the prelates' were the first outside events to affect him directly. Indirectly, he may have had his first contact with authoritarian government when his friend Alexander Gill was imprisoned and threatened with the pillory and loss of his ears (though the sentence, as finally carried out, was much lighter) for rejoicing too audibly at the assassination of the unpopular Duke of Buckingham in 1628. The only real political allusion in Milton's verse before his return from Italy was St Peter's digression in *Lycidas* on the corruption of the clergy. When he republished the poem in 1645, he added a note drawing attention to the prophetic quality of this passage. But prophets are notoriously hard to understand, and no critic has ever produced a definitive explanation of the lines which threaten an eventual punishment for the bad priests:

> But that two-handed engine at the door
> Stands ready to smite once, and smite no more.

He might be referring to either secular or ecclesiastical retribution, or even to the Last Judgment. It seems unlikely that he knew how close at hand the Puritan triumph really was.

He returned from Italy to find events moving with amazing speed. The King's unsuccessful attempt to force the Prayer Book and episcopacy on the Scots had become a focus for all the grievances built up over the ten years in which he had been trying to govern without consent of Parliament. When the Long Parliament finally met late in 1640, one of its first tasks was to debate a reform of Church government. A petition from the City of London asked it to abolish the bishops and the rest of the Church establishment 'root and branch'. To Milton, who still thought of himself as a victim of this establishment, the question of Church government was the most important one of the day. Laud had so thoroughly succeeded in uniting Church and State that there was no real separation between political and religious freedom. In the course of the 1640s there was a general movement from religious to political debate as it became clear that to alter the Church would also entail altering the government. Milton followed this movement to some extent but he always regarded religious freedom as the only true freedom, without which political freedom was valueless. Thus, against a background of anti-episcopal and pro-presbyterian feeling, he entered the controversy on how the English Church should be governed.

Probably during 1640 or 1641, he had renewed his acquaintance with his old tutor, Thomas Young, with whom he had kept in touch by letter since his childhood. Young and four other Presbyterian ministers—Stephen Marshall, Edmund Calamy, Matthew Newcomen, and William Spurstowe—combined their talents and initials in 1641 to produce an anti-episcopal pamphlet signed with the name of Smectymnuus. This pamphlet, to which Milton may have contributed a postscript, was mainly written by Young, and was an answer to Bishop Joseph Hall who, in his *Humble Remonstrance to the High Court of Parliament* had expressed his shock at the rapidity with which men seemed prepared to destroy the established order. Shortly after the publication of the Smectymnuan reply, Milton entered the debate on his own account, first with a pamphlet dealing with the issues of Church reform in general (*Of Reformation Touching Church Discipline in England*) and then with answers to specific writings by Hall and others on the episcopal side. Here he was able for the first time to diplay in public the tremendous store of scholarship which he had been accumulating since his departure from Cambridge. He also discovered that he had a talent for personal abuse. Unlike the comparatively moderate exchanges of Hall and the Smectymnuuns, Milton's pamphlets are full of extreme statements, unfair attacks on his opponents, and remarks like 'Wipe your fat corpulencies out of our light'. They are equally personal when he turns from satire to accounts of his own beliefs or hopes for the Church. It does not seem to have occurred to him that the general reader, when he bought a pamphlet on Church reform, might not particularly want to be told about the author's early tastes in reading, literary ambitions, or attitude to sex.

In spite of this lively material, Milton's anti-episcopal writings do not seem to have attracted much attention. Everyone was writing pamphlets in the early 1640s, encouraged by the ending of censorship, and Milton's probably got lost in the crowd. The subject of Church government, in any case, was soon exhausted. The debate on the Root and Branch Bill stretched into 1642, but was broken off by the coming of the Civil War.

It was not until 1649 that Milton again began writing on political subjects. From incidental remarks in *Areopagitica* (1644) we know that he watched the course of events with approval and welcomed the flood of political and religious pamphlets which followed the end of censorship; even Parliament's reimposition of licensing made little difference, since it was easy to evade the requirement; it has been suggested that this is why Milton's arguments against licensing in *Areopagitica* were not taken up by anyone else. Even so, the fact that the Presbyterians were prepared to silence hostile opinions in the same way that Laud had done confirmed Milton in his growing scepticism about a form of Church government which he had once admired, and perhaps also about Parliament itself.

At the outbreak of the war, he seems to have imagined that Parliament would construct a new society 'to which he would be able to make a valuable contribution. In a digression in *Reason of Church Government Urged* (1642) he offered to provide for the cultural and artistic life of such a society: he would write an epic, on a subject to be chosen by Parliament, or he would inaugurate a new, highly moral drama to replace the corruptions of the presentday stage, or he would compose songs of praise and triumph like those which had inspired the heroes of Greece and Rome. Between 1643 and 1645 he presented yet another series of contributions to the forthcoming social revolution, announcing a new concept of the Christian marriage. At least, this is what he thought he was doing. But his thoroughly Puritan belief in the sanctity of the true marriage led him to a conclusion which horrified his Puritan and non-Puritan readers: that a true marriage was possible only if one had the right to free oneself from an unworthy partner. At a time when the only valid grounds for divorce were adultery and non-consummation of the marriage, Milton was arguing on behalf of divorce for incompatibility; moreover, he felt that a husband should have the right to divorce his wife without calling in an outside opinion.

Milton later insisted that his turning from attacks on episcopacy to proposals for divorce law reform was perfectly consistent: he was defending freedom, religious in one case, domestic in another. There is no doubt, though, that he had personal reasons for his choice of subject. Early in the summer of 1642 he had married an eighteen-year-old girl, Mary Powell, who came from a Royalist family. Just before the outbreak of war in August she left him to visit her parents in Forest Hill, Oxfordshire, and did not return until 1645. Nothing definite is known as to how far this separation was the result of personal rather than political circumstances. Traffic between Royalist Oxford and Parliamentary London became increasingly dangerous in 1642 and was finally prohibited, so that she might not have been able to return even if she had wanted to. It was only after the Battle of Naseby, which meant the virtual collapse of the Royalist cause, that friends brought about a reconciliation between Milton and his wife. This domestic counterpart of the Civil War can only have enhanced Milton's feeling that his own cause and that of his country were inextricably bound up together.

Thus, the reception of his divorce pamphlets must have been a shock to him. They sold better than anything he had written yet, but for the wrong reasons. For the next twenty years at least, he was 'Milton the Divorcer' to people who knew nothing else about him; rumour had it that he had several wives still living. His former allies the Presbyterians wanted the pamphlets suppressed and in 1644 he was called for examination at the House of Lords, though no action was taken against him. Still more embarrassing were the few unbalanced readers who used the pamphlets as a justification for their own behaviour. Milton soon came to wish that he had not written in English for every fool to read. Hoping for a scholarly debate on the issue, he kept accumulating material and developing what he thought a watertight case, but the only published replies to his work were so contemptibly ill-informed that he got no pleasure from answering them. He began to be aware that his own need for self-fulfilment was always going to conflict both with the traditional laws of society and with the views of the average man. He became increasingly convinced that the truly superior man like himself was above all laws.

This belief lies behind even *Of Education* and *Areopagitica* (both 1644). Milton's interest in educational reform had nothing to do with a desire to spread literacy among the mass of the population, like the projects of Comenius, which Parliament had recently been considering. Rather, he proposed a sophisticated scheme by which an elite group of students would be educated under one roof from the ages of twelve to twenty-one. *Areopagitica* seems more egalitarian in its insistence that Truth may have more shapes than one, but Milton's eagerness to let all opinions contend in 'a free and open encounter' is based on his conviction that, given a fair hearing, he could bring others round to his opinions on all things that mattered.

Perhaps because of disgust at the reception of the divorce pamphlets, Milton left off publishing altogether between 1645 and 1649. His wife's return allowed him to settle down to a more normal domestic life while he busied himself with teaching and further research, especially in history. His next appearance in print, however, made it clear that he had not been growing any less revolutionary during those quiet years.

When Charles I was executed in 1649 only a small proportion of even the extremists in Parliament approved of the action. But Milton had come to the conclusion that the King, whom he had once regarded as an innocent victim of the bishops' overweening pride, was in fact a tyrant who had no right to obedience and whose

C

execution would be an act of justifiable self-defence on the part of the oppressed nation. During the King's trial he had been setting out his views in a pamphlet *On the Tenure of Kings and Magistrates*, which was published a month after the execution. Milton's cool appraisal of the current situation, his attack on the moderate Presbyterians who seemed to feel that they could carry on under a restored monarchy as if the past seven years had never happened, and above all his scholarship and polished literary style, must have caught the eye of someone in the new government. What it desperately needed, at this point, was a writer of stature who was prepared to write a defence of regicide.

Only a few days after the King's execution, the first blow had been struck against the Commonwealth by the secret publication of a book called *Eikon Basilike* (the King's image), which was supposed to have been written by Charles I in prison. This book gives an account, from the King's point of view, of the events between the summoning of the Long Parliament and the end of 1648, interspersed with prayers and meditations. Who actually wrote this pious work is still a puzzle; it seems to have been a bishop, possibly making use of some genuine writings by Charles himself. At any rate, it was a highly successful piece of propaganda, presenting the King both as a reasonable man destroyed by rabid extremists and as a saint who could say, 'If I must suffer a violent death, with My Saviour, it is but mortality crowned with martyrdom'. The frontispiece to the book (see p. oo) reinforced this impression by portraying him surrounded by religious symbols. King Charles the Martyr was rapidly becoming a cult hero and it became obvious to the new Council of State that *Eikon Basilike*, whether by the King or not, must be answered. A defence of the execution was also needed on the continent, where it had aroused intense horror.

In March the Council of State decided to offer Milton the position of Secretary for the Foreign Tongues. He was to attend some meetings of the Council, receive a salary of about £290 a year, and occupy rooms in Whitehall. His job would entail translating and in some cases composing the foreign correspondence of the new government; he was also to act as a kind of spokesman for England abroad. (Ironically, he also became a government censor in 1650.) Because of his eloquent writings on behalf of the Commonwealth Milton came to be closely identified with it in the minds of European statesmen, but in fact, as his most recent biographer points out, he had nothing to do with the Council's official decisions, and there is no real evidence, only a strong probability, that he ever met Cromwell.

His first and most immediate assignment was to set minds at rest in England by writing an answer to *Eikon Basilike*—a thankless task since it obliged him to attack a dead man. In a chapter-by-chapter analysis of the book, his main line of approach was to keep drawing attention to the contrast between the pious sentiments it expressed

Frontispiece to Eikon Basilike, *1649*

The Explanation of the EMBLEM.

Ponderibus *genus omne mali, probriq; gravatus,*
Vixq;ferenda ferens, Palma ut Depressa, resurgo.

Though clogg'd with *weights* of miseri
Palm-like Depressed, I higher rise.

Ac, *velut undarum Fluctus Ventiq;, furorem*
Irati Populi Rupes immota repello.

And as th' *unmoved Rock* out-brave's
The boist'rous *winds* and raging *waves:*
So *triumph I.* And shine more *bright*
In sad Affliction's Darksom night.

Clarior è tenebris, *cælestis stella, corusco,*
Victor & æternum-felici pace triumpho.

Auro Fulgentem *rutilo gemmisq; micantem,*
At curis Gravidam spernendo calco Coronam.

That *Splendid,* but yet *toilsom* Crown
Regardlesly I *trample* down.

Spinosam, *at ferri facilem, quo Spes mea* Christi
Auxilio, Nobis non est tractare molestum.

With joie I take this Crown of *thorn,*
Though *sharp,* yet *easie* to be born.

Æternum, *fixis fidei, sempérq;-beatum*
In Cælos oculis Specto, nobisq; paratam.

That *heav'nly* Crown, already mine;
I view with eies of Faith divine.

(præbet
Quod Vanum *est, sperno; quod* Christi Gratia
Amplecti studium est: Virtutis Gloria merces.

I slight *vain* things; and do embrace
Glorie, the just reward of *Grace.*

G. D

and the treacherous way in which, he felt, the King had behaved toward his subjects; Shakespeare's Richard III, he noted, could also cite Scripture for his purposes. But *Eikonklastes* was unable to live up to its name, which means image-breaker. It was too late to destroy the image of Charles I in the popular mind.

He was more successful on the continent, in that international scholarly community where he had felt so much at home when he travelled to Italy ten years earlier. A French writer, Claude Saumaise, published a formidable attack on the English regicides and Milton was commissioned to answer it. It seemed to him the moment for which he had been waiting all his life. Saumaise (or Salmasius, as he was known in the Latin-speaking world of scholarship) was famous for his learning and skill as a controversialist. It would be an honour to contest with him. Despite poor health and the increasing weakness of his eyes, Milton could not resist the opportunity to win international fame by putting all his scholarship, intelligence and eloquence at the service of a cause in which he so thoroughly believed. He called his reply to Salmasius's *Defence of the English King* a *Defence of the English People* (1651) and perhaps he really did believe that for once in his life he was speaking for his country, although the vast majority of his countrymen, given a free vote, would have chosen a restored monarchy rather than the commonwealth which Milton set out to glorify.

Milton became totally blind at about the same time as the *Defence* appeared, but it was generally believed, in Republican circles at least, that he had totally disgraced and destroyed the famous Salmasius, who died in 1653. It was said that before his death he had written a reply, but in the end this did not appear until after the Restoration, when it was impossible for Milton to answer it. Other royalist sympathizers kept him busy, however, first with another *Defence* (1654), then with a *Defence of Himself* (1655). What had begun as an ideological debate became a personal one, as is always likely to happen, and dealing in personalities brought out once again the harsh, satirical streak in Milton. Sometimes, though, he can be very funny, as when he breaks into Latin verses congratulating all fish on the forthcoming publication of Salmasius's reply, which will be used to wrap them and thus keep them warm in the cold winter months. When he turns from satire to panegyric, as in those passages describing the Commonwealth and its leaders, he shows himself capable of admiring moral courage in others as well as himself and expresses an eloquent and moving faith in the future of the country which he now regarded himself as having saved almost singlehanded.

The Council recognized the service he had done them and continued to pay him a salary even after he had been allowed a substitute in his secretarial post in 1655. The later years of the Commonwealth must have been depressing for him (he was living alone most of the time), but visits from foreigners who had admired his *Defences* provided some consolation. He was in fact better known abroad than in England. Perhaps this is why he decided to write his *Christian Doctrine*, which he began at about this time, in the international language. But it may be only that, remembering the fate of his divorce pamphlets, he wanted to ensure a learned audience for this attempt at a complete system of theology based exclusively on the Scriptures.

The first two English pamphlets which he published during the confused period after Cromwell's death in 1658 were on Church reform, not the more widely discussed question of what form of government should replace the Protectorate. Milton's interests were always more religious than political. However, he, like everyone else, soon found events moving so rapidly in the direction of a return to monarchy that it became essential to find a political alternative. Parliament seemed incapable of governing on its own, and was no longer a representative body anyway. In the circumstances hereditary kingship seemed preferable to chaos, and sentiment in favour of Charles II was growing.

Milton began frantically working at a proposed scheme of government which would end the anarchy without making way for dictatorship. He tried writing to General Monk who, as leader of the Parliamentary armies in Scotland, seemed to hold the key to the situation. But Monk had decided to use his power on the King's behalf. In February 1660 the original members of the Long Parliament (who had been excluded since 1648) were allowed to take their seats again. They were mostly Royalist and Presbyterian, and it became apparent that as soon as a free election was allowed they would decide to recall Charles II to his throne. The situation became, from Milton's point of view, increasingly hopeless, but he continued to modify his original proposals for a free commonwealth, to be governed by a perpetual Parliament. Rather than the return of a monarchy, he was prepared to have Monk himself as dictator; he was even willing, in the interests of national unity, to play down his belief in freedom of religious worship as the foundation of any just government.

Probably the most courageous thing Milton ever did was to publish *A Ready and Easy Way to Establish a Free Commonwealth*, whose second edition appeared only a month before the return of the King. He must have known that there was little hope of persuading anyone at this point. Other Republicans were already going into hiding. The fact that the second edition bore no printer's name on the titlepage (and Milton probably had to pay for the printing himself) shows how dangerous the expression of such views was now felt to be.

When Charles II entered London at the end of May, with church bells ringing and fountains running with wine in celebration, Milton must have expected to be put to death. He kept off the streets, living quietly with a friend in Bartholomew Close. What probably saved him from reprisals, for which he seemed an obvious target, was the

C R

DIEV ET MON DROIT

By the King.

A PROCLAMATION

For calling in, and suppressing of two Books written by *John Milton*; the one Intituled, *Johannis Miltoni Angli pro Populo Anglicano Defensio, contra Claudii Anonymi aliàs Salmasii, Defensionem Regiam*; and the other in answer to a Book Intituled, *The Pourtraicture of his Sacred Majesty in his Solitude and Sufferings.* And also a third Book Intituled, *The Obstructors of Justice,* written by *John Goodwin.*

CHARLES R.

Hereas John Milton, late of Westminster, in the County of Middlesex, hath Published in Print two several Books. The one Intituled, Johannis Miltoni Angli pro Populo Anglicano Defensio, contra Claudii Anonymi, aliàs Salmasii, Defensionem Regiam. And the other in Answer to a Book Intituled, The Pourtraicture of his Sacred Majesty in his Solitude and Sufferings. In both which are contained sundry Treasonable Passages against Us and Our Government, and most Impious endeavors to justifie the horrid and unmatchable Murther of Our late Dear Father, of Glorious Memory. And whereas John Goodwin, late of Coleman-street, London, Clerk, hath also published in Print, a Book Intituled, The Obstructors of Justice, written in defence of his said late Majesty. And whereas the said John Milton, and John Goodwin, are both fled, or so obscure themselves, that no endeavors used for their apprehension can take effect, whereby they might be brought to Legal Tryal, and deservedly receive condigne punishment for their Treasons and Offences.

Now to the end that Our good Subjects may not be corrupted in their Judgments, with such wicked and Traitrous principles, as are dispersed and scattered throughout the beforementioned Books, We, upon the motion of the Commons in Parliament now assembled, doe hereby streightly charge and Command, all and every Person and Persons whatsoever, who live in any City, Burrough, or Town Incorporate, within this our Kingdom of England, the Dominion of Wales, and Town of Berwick upon Tweed, in whose hands any of those Books are, or hereafter shall be, That they, upon pain of Our high Displeasure, and the consequence thereof, do forthwith, upon publication of this Our Command, or within Ten days immediately following, deliver, or cause the same to be delivered to the Mayor, Bayliffs, or other chief Officer or Magistrate, in any of the said Cities, Burroughs, or Towns Incorporate, where such person or persons so live, if living out of any City, Burrough, or Town Incorporate, then to the next Justice of Peace adjoyning to his or their dwelling, or place of abode; or if living in either of Our Universities, then to the Vice-Chancellor of that University where he or they do reside.

And in default of such voluntary delivery, which We do expect in observance of Our said Command, That then and after the time before limited, expired, the said Chief Magistrate of all and every the said Cities, Burroughs, or Towns Incorporate, the Justices of the Peace in their several Counties, and the Vice-Chancellors of Our said Universities respectively, are hereby Commanded to Seize and Take, all and every the Books aforesaid, in whose hands or possession soever they shall be found, and certifie the names of the Offenders unto Our Pivry Councel.

And We do hereby also give special Charge and Command to the said Chief Magistrates, Justices of the Peace, and Vice-Chancellors respectively, That they cause the said Books which shall be so brought unto any of their hands, or seized or taken as aforesaid, by vertue of this Our Proclamation, to be delivered to the respective Sheriffs of those Counties where they respectively live, the first and next Assizes that shall after happen. And the said Sheriffs are hereby also required, in time of holding such Assizes, to cause the same to be publickly burnt by the hand of the Common Hangman.

And We do further streightly Charge and Command, That no man hereafter presume to Print, Vend, Sell, or Disperse any the aforesaid Books, upon pain of Our heavy Displeasure, and of such further Punishment, as for their presumption in that behalf, may any way be inflicted upon them by the Laws of this Realm.

Given at Our Court at *Whitehall* the 13th day of *August*, in the Twelfth year of Our Reign, 1660.

LONDON, Printed by *John Bill* and *Christopher Barker*, Printers to the Kings most Excellent Majesty, 1660.

fact of his blindness; his enemies had always maintained that it was a punishment from God for his defence of regicide and, if this was true, there was no need for the state to take further action. Moreover, some members of the new Parliament, notably Andrew Marvell, were his friends. So, although *Eikonoklastes* and the *Defences* were condemned to be publicly burnt, and he himself was briefly imprisoned at the end of 1660, Milton was eventually granted a full pardon.

Forced out of political life, though never changing in his political beliefs, he was now free to write for himself alone. The hatreds stirred up by the Civil War died down with surprising rapidity, and Milton had many friends who were also members of the court of Charles II. There is a story that he was asked, and refused, to write on behalf of the new government. He may also have been called on, as an expert, to give some informal advice during an important divorce case in 1670. In 1673, a year before his death, he published his last pamphlet, pleading for tolerance among the various Protestant sects as the best way of combating the spread of 'Popery' in England. But these would have been brief interruptions in a generally quiet life. He married for the third time in 1663—happily, it seems—and the rest of his life belongs rather to literary than to political history.

Yet Milton himself would have made no distinction between the two. It is true that in one of his earlier pamphlets, *Reason of Church Government Urged*, he suggests that he regards himself primarily as a poet who, in writing prose, is using only his left hand. By the time he came to write as spokesman for the Commonwealth, however, he was convinced of the dignity of his role; his *Defence of the English People* seemed to him the equivalent of the great national epic which he had always meant to write. He had not sacrificed his eyesight to a petty slanging match, but to what he believed was the cause of true liberty. Even if he had never begun *Paradise Lost*, he might have felt that his political and religious works had achieved the goal toward which his whole life had been directed.

Literary career

Because there is such an extraordinary consistency in Milton's ambitions from his undergraduate days onwards, we are perhaps over-inclined to read all his works before *Paradise Lost* as if they were simply rough sketches for the great epic. In fact, until the outbreak of the Civil War, his literary career was not very different from that of any other young man of the period. He had begun writing verses as a child, as was typical, in an age when verse composition was part of the school curriculum; at Cambridge he acquired some reputation as a poet, as is shown by his being asked to contribute to the memorial volume for Edward King. At Cambridge also he produced his first published work, the epitaph on Shakespeare in the Second Folio edition of the plays in 1631. Other epitaphs by Milton would have circulated in manuscript: Latin ones on prominent churchmen; English ones on persons as diverse as the Roman Catholic Marchioness of Winchester and old Hobson, the horse-carrier, who was a familiar figure to all Cambridge undergraduates. These were the kinds of composition which any gifted student might have written.

Any student might have envied, also, the opportunity to compose verses for the entertainment presented by a noble family. Milton's *Arcades* (set to music by Henry Lawes) put him in a tradition of courtly poetry which Ben Jonson had made peculiarly his own. It addressed itself to members of the nobility with respect but not flattery, treating them as symbols of all that mankind, at its best, might be. At this stage of his life Milton may well have been looking for a patron. It would have been the natural course of action for anyone intending to make a career in literature. There is nothing of the conventional Puritan about the style of *L'Allegro* and *Il Penseroso*, and if *Comus* seems puritanical because of its emphasis on chastity and temperance one should remember that the subject matter of masques was always moralistic. What is more to the point is that four months before the production of *Comus*, the Puritan William Prynne had been put in the pillory and had his ears slit for writing an attack on masques and plays. In 1634 it must have seemed impossible that Milton and Prynne would ever find themselves on the same side.

Most of the poems which Milton assembled for publication in 1645 had been written before his journey to Italy. His book is presented in a lighthearted way that contrasts strangely with the time when it appeared. The frontispiece shows Milton in front of a pastoral scene, with verses in Greek underneath the picture expressing his disgust at the engraver's bad likeness (this was a joke on the engraver, who would have copied the lines without knowing what they meant). The titlepage informs the reader that the songs included in the book had already been set to music by Henry Lawes, 'one of his majesty's private music'. It is as if Milton were declaring that his poetry belonged to a completely separate world from that of the prose pamphlets which he had been writing during the past four years. Perhaps he was consciously rounding off a period of his life and putting his youthful work behind him.

He did, however, put the *Ode on the Morning of Christ's Nativity* at the beginning of the English poems, as if to establish the fact of his dedication, from earliest youth, to sacred subjects. Following this, he added rhymed translations of the 114th and 136th psalms, done at the age of fifteen, and his two attempts, both unsuccessful, to celebrate other events in the life of Christ as he had done his nativity. But the two works which he placed at the end of the English poems, both because of their length and (probably) because he rightly regarded them as his finest, were done to order. *Comus* (which was not called by that name until the eighteenth century) was specifically designed for a single performance in 1634 by the children of the Earl of Bridgewater; *Lycidas* was last in a memorial volume of verses by Cambridge acquaintances of Edward King, a young poet studying for the priesthood, who was drowned in 1637. The section of Latin poems, similarly, ended with a pastoral elegy on Milton's friend Charles Diodati. Both elegies give a sense of bidding farewell not only to the friend but also to the pastoral convention in which they were written.

Pastoral was traditionally the medium in which a young man wrote before going on to produce his mature work. In the early 1640s Milton was still thinking aloud as to what that work should be. It is possible that he thought Parliament might become his patron; some such hope may have lain behind his brief outline of his literary ambitions in *Reason of Church Government Urged*. He had two main plans, one for an epic and one for a tragedy, but both were intended to be 'doctrinal and exemplary to a nation'. No doubt for this reason, he looked for the Christian hero of his epic among kings and knights 'before the conquest'—before the Norman Conquest, that is, when, so the Parliamentarians believed, the ancient liberties of England had been destroyed by foreign laws. According to the Latin poem he addressed to Manso, his favourite idea was the story of Arthur before he became king. The theme may have attracted him because Arthur was one of the few British heroes known outside Britain. At the same time, he began making lists of possible subjects, biblical and historical, which might have a good effect on an audience's morals. Wherever possible he notes how a character may be held up as a warning against such vices as drunkenness or lust. He also includes a list of 'Scotch stories, or rather British of the north parts', presumably to teach the English more about their Scottish Presbyterian allies in the war. The sketches for their treatment show that what he had in mind was something between opera and Greek tragedy, making a good deal of use of the chorus, the narration of offstage events, and supernatural characters. *His* version of *Macbeth*, for instance, would have begun with the meeting of Malcolm and Macduff; the murder of Duncan would not have been shown, but narrated instead by his ghost.

At some point Milton decided against the idea of an Arthurian epic, perhaps because his extensive reading in history had made him doubt the truth of the whole legend. He concentrated instead on the one subject about whose truth he had no doubt. But the fall of Adam was still a dramatic rather than an epic subject for him. According to Edward Phillips, who was Milton's pupil in the 1640s, Satan's first soliloquy from Book IV of *Paradise Lost* was written as the opening speech of a religious tragedy. If Milton had carried out this plan, the fall of Adam and Eve would have taken place offstage, between acts III and IV, and they would not have appeared in person until afterwards. Milton's awareness of the difficulty of presenting the characters onstage in their unfallen and naked state suggests that he was thinking of the tragedy as a work to be performed and not merely read. Parliament closed the London theatres in 1642 and they did not reopen until the Restoration, but musical performances were still allowed (the first English opera was performed under the Commonwealth). Whether or not Milton originally intended his *Adam Unparadised* to include music—like the Greek tragedy, the English masque, and the recent Italian operas—he must have been convinced that no government could prohibit so obviously instructive an entertainment.

His attitude had changed by the time he came to write *Samson Agonistes*, designed to be read rather than seen (see p. 125 for discussion of the dating of this play). Drama no longer seemed to him the best medium for the story of Adam's fall. He saw more in it than could be comprehended in a play, unlike Andreini, the author of an Italian opera on the same subject, who complained of the difficulty of stretching into five acts the simple business of eating an apple. To Milton that simple action had been the turning point in man's fate and had to be presented in the context of all human history since the fall. In particular, though critics may have stressed this point too much, the fate of the Commonwealth may have seemed to him proof that fallen man could never enjoy freedom even when, as in the 1650s, all things seemed to favour him. Since the day when Adam had made the wrong choice, it had become impossible for man ever to make the right one.

Parliament's decision to recall Charles II must have seemed the confirmation of this view, though probably Milton had begun the writing of *Paradise Lost* earlier, at a time when his blindness and the dying down of the Salmasius controversy had relieved him of most of his government work and left him more leisure in which to compose. It was difficult, certainly, for a blind man to write an epic poem, but not so difficult as a work of research, which might require untrained readers to stumble through scholarly volumes (Milton's daughters are supposed to have been taught to read aloud in languages they did not understand) and more or less capable scribes to take down pertinent quotations from them. Milton's memory had always been good. He could retain forty or fifty newly composed lines in his head until someone was available to write them at his dictation. Later he had them read back to him, and made corrections. *Paradise Lost* was, above all, a poem meant to be *heard*.

This slow business of composition (perhaps made even slower by Milton's belief that he could compose with facility only in autumn and winter) may have lasted for about seven years. Thomas Ellwood, a Quaker friend of Milton's, who found him a house in Buckinghamshire at the time of the 1665 plague in London, read the completed poem in that year. Publication may have been held up by the Great Fire of 1666, which destroyed many of the bookshops and publishing

Milton's cottage at Chalfont St. Giles

houses clustered around old St Paul's. It finally appeared, in ten books, in 1667. Milton made only £15 in all from this and the revised 1674 edition (in twelve books), but that was a reasonable amount for the period. The poem seems to have had a quiet success.

Ellwood, who was perhaps the first person to read *Paradise Lost*, believed himself responsible for the shorter epic which followed it. His comment, when he returned the manuscript, had been, 'Thou hast said much here of Paradise Lost, but what hast thou to say of Paradise Found?' Milton was silent for a while, then changed the subject. When Ellwood saw him again, some time after his return to London, 'he shewed me his second poem, called *Paradise Regained*, and in a pleasant tone said to me, "This is owing to you; for you put it into my head by the question you put to me at Chalfont, which before I had not thought of." '

Both Ellwood's and Milton's words were spoken 'pleasantly'— that is, almost jokingly—and probably ought not to be taken too seriously. *Paradise Lost* is certainly not incomplete as it stands, and Ellwood would have been very stupid if he had missed the point of the conclusion with its promise of a double redemption, both through the sufferings of Christ and through man's own efforts to win his 'Paradise within'. But Milton may have seen in Ellwood's words a graceful suggestion that he should now think of a New Testament epic. Long ago, in listing the various kinds of literary work which he thought worth attempting, he had noted that, although the classical epic was usually a large-scale work, the Book of Job might be described as a 'brief epic'. This new form posed new and interesting problems, particularly that of retaining epic dignity in a work involving only one episode and a small number of characters. According to Edward Phillips, he came to prefer his short epic to the longer one, and was annoyed when people, then as now, let it be overshadowed by its predecessor.

Whether because of the growing esteem for *Paradise Lost* or because Milton's former notoriety was a good selling-point, he was able, before his death in 1674, to find publishers for nearly everything he had ever written, even his Latin grammar, handbook on the art of logic, and academic exercises. *Paradise Regained* and *Samson Agonistes* were published together in 1671; a new edition of his poems came out in 1673, including most of the Civil War sonnets except those dedicated to prominent Republicans; finally, there was the revised edition of *Paradise Lost* in 1674. What little still remained in manuscript was in print by 1700.

There was one exception: the *Christian Doctrine*. Having reluctantly given up the hope of publishing this statement of his religious beliefs during his lifetime, Milton finally bequeathed it, and the responsibility for publishing it, to Daniel Skinner, a former pupil who had also acted as his secretary. This young man soon found his legacy too hot to handle. Warned that his career would suffer otherwise, he gave up his rather feeble attempt at carrying out Milton's wishes and the manuscript then disappeared until it was found in a Whitehall cupboard in the nineteenth century.

Many of those who visited Milton in his last years were literary men. Marvell, of course, had been his friend and assistant during the Commonwealth period. He wrote a spirited and sensible defence of Milton in 1673, when one of his own literary enemies had dragged his friend's name into the quarrel, and complimentary verses by him appeared in the 1674 edition of *Paradise Lost*. Dryden, whom Marvell ridicules in those verses, was also an acquaintance and admirer of Milton's. There is a tradition that on one of his visits he asked, and received, permission to turn *Paradise Lost* into a musical entertainment in heroic couplets, but Milton, who died peacefully toward the end of 1674, was spared the experience of reading *The State of Innocence*, published in 1678 but never performed. Its blend of rational scepticism and sensuality is by no means unattractive, but it belongs to a different age from Milton's. The first words of Dryden's Adam, on awakening to life, are a paraphrase of Descartes's 'I think, therefore I am'.

Dryden's was the first of many adaptations, including several in rhyme. One can imagine what Milton would have thought of a 1699 version, supposedly designed for lady readers, of three extracts from the poem in heroic couplets. The entire argument between Eve and Satan in Book IX, so crucial to his concept of reason and free choice, was here reduced to

> And now persuaded by a long dispute,
> She boldly tastes of the forbidden fruit.

There were other tributes which he would have found more gratifying, such as the translations of *Paradise Lost* into Latin, the illustrated 1688 edition with Dryden's verses declaring that Milton combined the best qualities of Homer and Virgil, and the annotated edition of 1695 which gave him the status of a classic. After the Revolution of 1688 it became possible to think of him not only as a Regicide and Divorcer but also as a man who had prepared the way for the liberty of the post-Stuart era. His poetry sometimes got lost, as it still does, behind his politics and religion. Nevertheless, if the last part of his life had a serenity which had been lacking for many years before, it was probably because Milton, with his lifetime's ambition fulfilled, could foresee the acclaim which would follow and know that he deserved it.

Appearance and character

Milton himself is the main source of most of our information about him. He was certain that he would be remembered by posterity, and wanted to be sure that posterity got its facts right. Moreover, he believed that the moral rightness of a cause was inseparable from that of the men who upheld it. Thus, even more than other controversialists, he took personal attacks on himself very seriously and made a point of refuting them in detail. His most elaborate self-portrait, for instance, was written in the *Second Defence* (1654) as an answer to a writer who had described him as an ugly monster, 'feeble, bloodless, and pinched':

> I admit that I am not tall, but my stature is closer to the medium than to the small . . . neither am I especially feeble . . . when my age and manner of life required it, I was not ignorant of how to handle or unsheathe a sword, nor unpractised in using it each day. . . . Today I possess the same spirit, the same strength, but not the same eyes. And yet they have as much the appearance of being uninjured, and are as clear and bright, without a cloud, as the eyes of men who see most keenly. . . . In my face, than which he says there is 'nothing more bloodless', still lingers a color exactly opposite to the bloodless and pale, so that although I am past forty, there is scarcely anyone to whom I do not seem younger by about ten years. Nor is it true that either my body or my skin is shriveled.

Though Milton prefaces this account by saying that he does not care whether he is handsome or not, he obviously cared enough about his appearance to ask others to reassure him that he had not changed during his two years of blindness. Yet even this apparently trivial matter was weighted with moral significance for him. There was a widespread belief that the face was a reliable indication of a man's character: a pale complexion, for instance, was supposed to be a sign that its owner had a melancholy temperament. Milton is anxious to make it clear that he, on the contrary, fits the description of the 'sanguine' type—that is, that his political views are the expression of a well-balanced mind, not the ravings of an embittered neurotic.

The insistence on his youthful appearance shows another constant preoccupation of Milton's, also evident in his careful dating of his early poems to draw attention to their precocity. He never seems to have got over the fact that he was something of a child prodigy, and, because he looked younger than his actual age (see, for instance, the portrait of him as a Cambridge student on p. 8), he probably kept this sort of reputation well into adult life. The result is that, in an age when men were expected to mature early, Milton took a surprisingly long time growing up. On the one hand, he worried about not accomplishing anything in his twenties; on the other, he seemed to feel that he was too young at twenty-nine to compose a fitting elegy for Lycidas and, at thirty-three, that he had been drawn into religious controversy in his 'green years', before he was fully prepared for the task. (It is true, however, that the formal course of study for a degree in divinity was extremely long, and that Milton held the traditional view that wisdom could come only with age. Later on, he was to refer to Sir Henry Vane, who was forty, as 'young in years'.)

If Milton's image of himself in his thirties was that of a young and still inexperienced man, this is partly because of the standard of maturity and knowledge which he had set himself. He believed that the true poet was divinely inspired, but he also believed in the parable of the talents, which showed that God expected man to use and improve the gifts he had been granted. His ambitions were the highest that any writer of the time could have, and they required him to be not only the most talented and learned of men but also the most virtuous. 'He who would not be frustrate of his hope to write well hereafter in laudable things, ought himself to be a true poem,' he wrote in his *Apology for Smectymnuus*. And there is a sense in which his whole life can be seen as a self-conscious work of art.

Milton is so anxious to portray himself as a man of reason, whose life was carefully planned, that to modern readers he is likely to seem almost inhuman, not to say self-righteous. He did not really live on so completely rational a level as he tries to make out, and one may learn a good deal from what he leaves out of his autobiographical writings. He writes at some length about his education, his reading, his literary ambitions and political activity, but never mentions, even in his letters, the three-year period of separation from his first wife or such private griefs as the death of his only son in infancy. It is from others that we learn most of the attractive humanizing details about him: that he liked to sing, even during fits of the gout; that he sometimes composed verses while lying in bed in the morning; that he was cheerful and 'the life of the conversation'; that he rolled his 'r's (perhaps in the Italian manner?). Only in his letters does one find an occasional example of humour which is not hostile in tone, for instance his comment that the exorbitantly high price of an Atlas, which he had enquired about from a friend in Holland, must refer not to the book but to the mountain of that name. But most of the time his letters are literary compositions rather than familiar glimpses.

We know that the young Milton loved chivalric romances, fairy tales, and books about faraway places. When such a person writes of the importance of subordinating passion to reason it may be because he finds it difficult to be as completely rational as he would like. Much of what looks like self-righteousness in Milton's work probably is the result of a deep psychological need. There were two ways in which he could have taken his blindness, for instance. One was the way in which the Royalists took it: as God's judgment on the man who had justified the killing of God's anointed king. This would, of course, have made life unbearable to him. He chose the other alternative, thinking of himself as one set apart from other men, in the company of the great epic poet Homer, the all-knowing prophet Tiresias, the hero Samson, and the philosopher-scientist Galileo. Only *Samson* might be seen as the expression of something like self-doubt, and even there the hero is completely justified at last,

> With God not parted from him, as was feared,
> But favouring and assisting to the end
>
> (1719–20).

Without the obstinate faith in himself which long outlasted his other ideals, he might well have given up. His courage was based on an absolute certainty that he was right.

2 Scientific background

Milton and seventeenth-century science

The seventeenth century was the age when science as we know it first came into existence. At the time when Milton was growing up, although there had been many English followers of Copernicus in the previous century, the average educated man still held a view of the universe which derived from Aristotle (fourth century B.C.) and medical theory was based on the work of Galen (second century A.D.). By the end of the century, most of the scientific references in *Paradise Lost* were so out of date as to give the impression that Milton was parading esoteric theories instead of common knowledge. When Augustan critics complained of Milton's ostentation of his learning, they did not mean the literary allusions but the scientific ones.

The 'Scientific Revolution' which brought about this rapid change of attitude was in fact part of the same spirit which, as we shall see in the next chapter, also made itself felt in political and religious matters, and was eventually to have its effect on literature as well. One might describe this spirit as an insistence on seeing things as they really were, not as they had always been thought to be, or as they ought ideally to be, or as they had to be in order to prove a philosophical point. In other words, the emphasis was to be on practice rather than theory, on the nature of the object being looked at rather than the ingenuity of the person looking at it. At the beginning of the century, Sir Francis Bacon, in his *Advancement of Learning* (1605) and *Novum Organum* (1620), laid down a programme for research, based on observation and cooperation between researchers. Early in the Restoration, the Royal Society set about the implementation of these principles. The Society was chartered by Charles II but its special emphasis on practical work and intellectual democracy was essentially Puritan in spirit and many seventeenth-century scientists had Puritan sympathies.

The ideal, for Bacon and the founder members of the Royal Society, was that truth would be found by compiling the labours of many men. In practice it was not so simple. Both the Copernican theory and Harvey's account of the circulation of the blood, for instance, were first stated as hypotheses and only proved later by observation, after the instruments had been invented that enabled observations to be made. The great leaps forward still depended on the individual genius and not the hardworking committee. Nevertheless, the scientific ideal of cooperation was to some extent an anti-individualistic one, particularly in its effect on English prose. Scientists needed a common language, clear and unambiguous; a highly personal, emotional or poetic style was a liability when the main aim was rapid communication of knowledge. Thomas Sprat, whose *History of the Royal Society* was published in the same year as *Paradise Lost*, optimistically declared that the new science would be

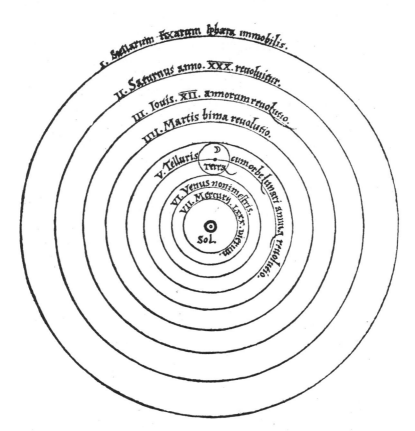

Copernicus, The Spheric Structure of the Universe, *1543*

a fresh source of poetic material. Milton's epic does indeed make use of science in a highly imaginative way, and suspends judgment on doubtful points with a detachment worthy of the Society, but his style, with its deliberate ambiguities, serious puns, and sliding syntax, is as far removed as anything could be from the precision which was soon to be a characteristic of poetry as well as prose.

As a young man Milton was something of a supporter of Baconian science. At Cambridge he was an anti-traditionalist, and the educational manifesto which he published in 1644 recommends supplementing the theoretical side of study with talks by 'hunters, fowlers, fishermen, shepherds, gardeners, apothecaries', and so on. Nevertheless, the theory came first. And, though he himself gave instruction in geography, mathematics, agronomy, botany, anatomy, and astronomy, he did so in the traditional way, that is, by having the students read Latin and Greek texts on these subjects. There is not much evidence in his writings of the direct observation which was the essential feature of the new science.

But this is hardly surprising. Despite his early interest, Milton was almost completely cut off from the world of science after 1649. Busy with his writings on behalf of the government, and with his eyesight progressively worsening until the total blindness of 1652, he was never again able to have more than a hearsay knowledge of what was going on. Thus, though he heard about microscopes, for instance (he had friends in the Royal Society), he could never have seen one. When Satan is showing Christ all the kingdoms of the world from a mountain top, he tells him,

> Many a fair edifice besides, more like
> Houses of Gods (so well I have disposed
> My airy microscope) thou mayst behold
> Outside and inside both

> (IV.55–8)

—which suggests that Milton imagined the instrument to be a device for seeing through things rather than magnifying them. Similarly, he does not seem to have known about the most important medical triumph of the century, Harvey's theory of the circulation of the blood (published in 1628), nor about the later microscope work which confirmed it by discovering the capillaries whose existence Harvey had postulated.

On the other hand, whether or not he ever looked through Galileo's telescope, Milton seems to have been fascinated by it. Classical and medieval descriptions of the world as seen from above in dreams or visions always note the smallest details despite the tremendous distance separating the observer from his object. This same combination of extreme distance with extreme clarity is seen in the account of Raphael's view of earth from the heavens, but Milton justifies it by comparing it with the view through a telescope:

> From hence, no cloud, or, to obstruct his sight,
> Star interposed, however small he sees,
> Not unconform to other shining globes,
> Earth and the garden of God, with cedars crowned
> Above all hills. As when by night the glass
> Of Galileo, less assured, observes
> Imagined lands and regions in the moon . . .

> (V. 257–63).

Though he didn't believe in astrology—at least, not in so far as it implied a denial of free will—he had his horoscope drawn up at some time around 1650. It looks as if he also took note of such phenomena as eclipses and comets, both of which were in fact visible over Britain in the year when he went totally blind. The study of the stars was traditionally a symbol for intellectual arrogance as well as impracticability, but Milton also points out in his *Christian Doctrine* that there is good biblical precedent for it in the observations of the three Magi, which led them to the infant Christ.

42

At times, one feels, Milton actually sees contemporary science as a joke. Raphael suggests that perhaps God has left His universe mysterious in order to have a good laugh at the wild theories men will devise in order to explain it. There seems no doubt of Milton's admiration for Galileo, the only contemporary figure mentioned in *Paradise Lost*, and yet there is sly humour in his account of Satan landing on the surface of the sun,

> a spot like which perhaps
> Astronomer in the sun's lucent orb
> Through his glazed optic tube yet never saw
>
> (III, 587–90).

Throughout Satan's voyage through the cosmos, Milton almost teasingly avoids committing himself as to its structure: Satan flies past stars which might possibly be inhabited (another subject of speculation in Milton's time), but does not stop to find out whether they are or not.

Even in more serious contexts we are offered alternative views of natural phenomena. When the sun 'sets', we can decide for ourselves

> whether the bright orb,
> Incredible how swift, had thither rolled
> Diurnal, or this less voluble earth
> By shorter flight to the east, had left him there
> Arraying with reflected purple and gold
> The clouds that on his western throne attend
>
> (IV, 592–7).

Satan's lines about earth in Book IX seem at first sight to be an endorsement of the geocentric view:

> Terrestrial heaven, danced round by other heavens
> That shine, yet bear their bright officious lamps,
> Light above light, for thee alone, as seems,
> In thee concentring all their precious beams
> Of sacred influence
>
> (IX, 104–7).

But even here, Milton is trying to have it both ways. It may seem unlikely that Satan, after the amount of space travel he has done, should make a mistake about the position of Earth in the cosmos, but that parenthetical 'as seems' can only mean that either he or Milton is reserving judgment about the literal accuracy of the whole description. It is possible that Milton wants to contrast Satan's easy acceptance of appearances with the much subtler reasoning of which Adam, with far less experience, has already shown himself capable. But the main value of the passage is poetic and emotional. For Satan, the apparent centrality of the earth emphasizes the important place of man in God's eyes, contrasted with the remoteness and isolation of Hell.

A few details of Satan's journey do, however, indicate that Milton is thinking in terms of the earlier view of the cosmos: the universe has an outer shell hard enough for Satan to walk upon, and is seen, at the end of Book II, hanging from heaven on a golden chain. But, it has to be remembered that Milton is writing about the world before the fall of man, not about any real world, Ptolemaic or Copernican, that we have ever known. Before the fall, it was believed, there were no harsh changes of season, because the sun's path was exactly along the equator instead of at an angle to it. The mountains were as high as the seas were deep, thus preserving the regular spherical form of the world beneath its surface variety. Milton describes in Book X how, at God's command, the sun (or the earth— as usual, he gives alternatives) is tilted so as to produce freezing winters and burning summers in place of the perpetual spring of Eden.

Symmetry and harmony were signs of good, their absence a sign of evil. But each discovery of the new science took away something from the symmetrical and harmonious medieval picture of the circle-based universe. For this reason, perhaps, most of Milton's specific references to scientific discoveries are attached to Satan. The lines in Book III describing Satan as a spot on the sun have already been quoted (p. 43). Galileo's discovery in 1613 of dark patches on the surface of the sun was received with alarm because everything above the moon was believed to be unchangeable and perfect, unlike the changeable, imperfect earth. That Satan himself should be seen as a sunspot is thus appropriate: it is because of him that evil, and therefore change and decay, has been introduced into the world. Similarly, the famous comparison of his shield to the moon (I.284–91) says more than the obvious fact that both objects are large, round and shiny. Like the moon, and like Satan himself, the shield is of 'ethereal temper', but as we draw nearer to it through the 'optic glass' it turns out, like the moon, to be a 'spotty Globe'. Naturally, a shield that has been carried in battle would be as battered as the surface of the moon now appeared to be, but in both cases the spots and irregularities represent a loss of perfection, as do the 'deep scars of thunder' which the archangel himself bears on his face.

Thus Milton was able to use both the new and the old astronomy to point a contrast between the fallen and unfallen world. The occasional ambiguity of his treatment may be only partly intentional. Like other writers of his time and later, Milton could not help using a poetic vocabulary based on the outdated cosmology. The old science still lingers in our language: we talk of 'sunrise' and 'sunset', for example. Probably most people nowadays who speak of 'being out of spirits' or of 'a sanguine temperament' or of 'spheres of influence' have no idea of what these terms really mean. Yet they derive from the same world view as the more exotic-seeming 'epicycle' and 'primum mobile'. The old science had permeated every part of life as the new still has not. However wrong its basic premises may have been, the result of its elaborate pattern of analogies between God, the universe and man was so beautiful as to seem logically inevitable. Its belief in the unity of all creation shows even in the names it gave to the universe (the *macrocosm* or great world) and to man himself (the *microcosm* or little world). The great and little worlds were intimately related, and to understand one it was necessary also to understand the other.

The macrocosm

One reason why the traditional earth-centred view of the universe lasted so long was that, up to a point, it did work. Men could use the old astronomy to navigate by the stars, keep a calendar, tell time, and predict eclipses. But its real value was not so much practical as philosophical and even emotional, which is probably why classical authors who suggested a heliocentric hypothesis were unable to make much headway.

The 'great world' of the universe had been made for man; that was why earth was at the centre. It had been made by God, and was therefore created perfect, which meant unchanging, since only an imperfect being needs to change. It was based on the most perfect of forms, which was the sphere—perfect, because it had neither beginning nor end and was complete in itself. Christian and classical writers shared a fascination with the spherical symbol so strong that even Copernicus could not get rid of the concept of a spherical universe. It was not until the work of Kepler (1571–1630) that the planets were found to move in ellipses rather than circles. Curiously enough, it was at this period also that the oval replaced the circle as the dominant form in art and architecture. It is as if no scientific idea could be accepted until it met an aesthetic need.

The plate on p. 47 shows a picture of the universe which derives essentially from Aristotle, though modified by Christian writers to bring it into accord with the Bible. Aristotle believed that the universe was eternal, whereas the Bible speaks of its eventual destruction at the second coming of Christ. Here, as so often, the explanation for the contradiction was that the fall of man had introduced decay into a hitherto changeless universe. This decay affected only the earth and the sublunary world (that is, below the moon), which was made up of a combination of the four elements: earth, water, air, and fire. Each of these had a sphere of its own. It is typical of the medieval attitude to science that maps should include a sphere of fire, for which there was no visible evidence, simply because it seemed logically necessary. Each of the elements was supposed to be the result of a combination of the four qualities: hot, cold, moist and dry. Water, for instance, was cold and moist;

when it became hot instead, it turned into another element, air.

Both Plato and Aristotle were basically in agreement about the nature of the world beneath the moon. They differed, however, about the relationship between sublunary and translunary substance (that of the realms beyond the moon). For Aristotle there was a complete break between the two: he thought that the planets and their spheres were made of a fifth essence (or *quintessence*) completely different from the four elements or from anything below the moon. Plato, on the other hand, had said that the translunary world was made up of the quintessence of the four elements—that is, some special rarefield combination of them—and was thus continuous with the lower world, although superior to it. The distinction between these two views was important because it affected man's view of his place in relation to God and the angels. Milton preferred the Platonic idea, which makes man and earth part of the same stream of life as the inhabitants of heaven.

Above the moon were the seven planets (which included the sun and moon), the sphere of the fixed stars, the 'crystalline sphere', and the Primum Mobile or First Mover. Beyond that was Heaven. Plato's universe did not include the concept of a First Mover; he thought that the planets were gods and moved of their own accord, guided by what he called 'intelligences'. Some Christian writers also use this theory and identify 'intelligences' with angels (Milton's Uriel, the angel in the sun, seems rather like one of these).

To understand Aristotle's very different theory, it is necessary to realize that he did not believe there was such a thing as empty space in the heavens: matter was continuous. The spheres, for him, were not imaginary lines like the planetary orbits of our science, but the layers of an onion. Obviously, they were not as solid as an onion. The closest analogy for Aristotle's universe would be a bowl of transparent jelly in which the heavenly bodies are embedded like cherries. They have two motions: one is that of their own spheres, which carries them along at varying rates of speed, while the other, much faster, one is that of the bowl itself—the Primum Mobile—which carries them in the opposite direction to that of the spheres. It was easy enough for Christians to identify the Primum Mobile with their God. He was the hand that turned the bowl.

Clearly, the existence of the Primum Mobile made it unnecessary to assume the presence of intelligences or angels in the spheres, since the stars and planets, being fixed in their places, needed no one to manoeuvre them. Nevertheless there were some features of the Platonic universe which were so attractive that Christian writers, including Milton, were unwilling to part with them. In particular, there was the belief in the music of the spheres, which Plato got from the mathematician-philosopher Pythagoras. The theory was that each of the spheres as it turned produced a musical note and that the combination of all of them, moving at equal distances from one another though at different speeds, created a sublime harmony

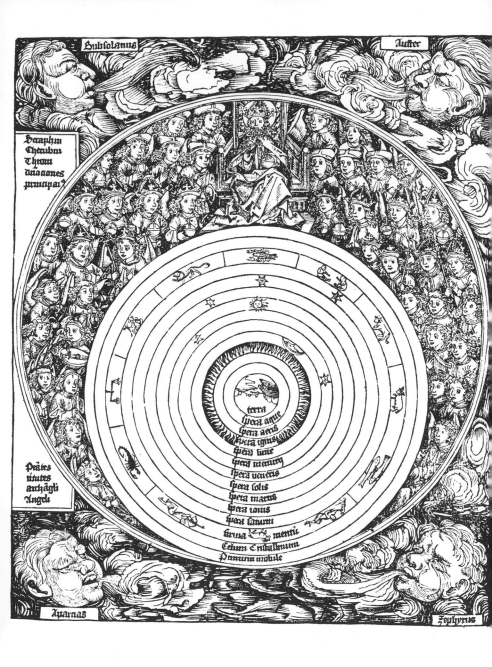

Medieval cosmos with earth at centre, from Nuremberg Chronicle, *1493*

which unfortunately was unaudible to mortal ears. Christian writers related the music of the spheres to the angelic songs which the Bible so frequently mentions, and explained their inaudibility as yet another consequence of the fall of man. Milton's *Ode on the Morning of Christ's Nativity* shows a typical Renaissance fusion of the two classical concepts of the universe in a Christian context: his 'crystal spheres' sound Aristotelean, but they are making Platonic music to celebrate the birth of Christ.

Beyond the planets lay the sphere of the fixed stars, so called because it was believed that they had no motion of their own but were moved all at once by the sphere in which they lay embedded. When Arab astronomers in the Middle Ages discovered that the stars did in fact move, though much less perceptibly than the planets, they tried to account for the fact by postulating the existence of another sphere just within the shell of the Primum Mobile. This 'crystalline sphere' is one of the most confusing components of the medieval universe. Its existence was debated by astronomers, but Milton seems to have believed in it, at least for poetic purposes. Christian thinkers liked to identify it with the mysterious 'waters above the earth' which, in the Genesis account of the Creation, were supposed to have been separated from those on the earth. Hence, the crystalline sphere was thought of as in some way being liquid; Milton calls it an ocean and describes it as cushioning the rest of the universe against the pressure of Chaos outside (*PL* VII. 261–73). According to this view, the sphere of the fixed stars would be equivalent to the Biblical 'firmament in the midst of the waters' (Genesis, 1:6).

As this addition of an extra sphere shows, the Aristotelean view of the cosmos underwent a number of changes designed to reconcile it with observed facts. The technical name for this act of reconciliation was 'saving appearances' and its most famous practitioner was the Egyptian astronomer Ptolemy (second century A.D.), whose name is frequently attached to the medieval cosmos. Essentially, his contribution was a device for reconciling the circle-based universe of Aristotle with observations which indicated irregular motions of the stars and planets. He suggested that an apparently irregular planet might nevertheless be regarded as moving around a circle whose centre did not coincide with the earth's (this was an 'eccentric') or around a point on the circumference of another sphere (this motion was an 'epicycle'). Thus it was mathematically possible to keep the circle as the basis of the planetary system, but only at the expense of simplicity. God will laugh, Raphael says, to see how men will

> build, unbuild, contrive
> To save appearances, how gird the sphere
> With centric and eccentric scribbled o'er,
> Cycle and epicycle, orb in orb
> (*PL* VIII, 81–4).

Yet 'saving appearances' was also the principle to which Copernicus appealed in putting forth his own hypothesis; he did not offer it as an absolute truth, but only as a simpler explanation than Ptolemy's. It was not until the observations of Tycho Brahe, Galileo and Kepler began to confirm his hypothesis that it became impossible to treat it simply as matter for speculation.

There is one final point to note about the medieval universe. By giving it a shape, philosophers necessarily made it finite. But there was nothing cosy about its limitations; it was still thought of as immensely vast. In the Christian view, God and his Heaven lay outside the universe. Theologians liked to describe God in terms of the perfect circle, but his infinitude contradicted all attempts to give a shape to it. A famous definition calls him 'a circle whose circumference is nowhere and whose centre is everywhere'. Thus the finite was surrounded by the infinite. In the same way, Milton sets his universe in infinite space, with Chaos beating at its walls, and also sets the Garden of Eden in the midst of a wilderness which constantly threatens to encroach on it. Here, as so often, macrocosm and microcosm correspond.

The microcosm

As the earth was at the centre of the world, so man was at the centre of the earth. Writers were used to finding analogies between microcosm and macrocosm, particularly the obvious ones implied in the pseudo-science of astrology. A man might derive his personality, in part at least, from the planet he was born under, hence the terms 'mercurial', 'saturnine', 'jovial', although orthodox Christianity held that it was possible to overcome the influence of the stars by faith. Doctors consulted an almanack before deciding when to bleed a patient or perform an operation, since different signs of the zodiac were thought to control different parts of the body and to be more or less favourable at different times.

It was reasonable to suppose that a universe made for man would contain everything that man needed to cure him. Beasts were believed to have an instinctive sense of which herbs were medicinal for them, and the sixteenth-century Paracelsus, half-scientist, half quack, taught men to look for what he called the 'signatures' in nature, which were supposed to show the uses to which particular plants and minerals were to be put. For instance, he suggested that the walnut must be good for diseases of the brain, since its shape was similar. A belief in the mysterious unity of all things led some doctors even in the seventeenth century to practice 'sympathetic magic': in order to treat a wound, they would anoint the weapon which had made it.

Man, like his universe, was said to be composed of the four

qualities and the four elements, and he derived his nature from the particular combination of these which predominated within him. The man who wished to care for his own health, physical or mental, needed to balance by careful diet any excess of heat or cold, moisture or dryness, in his constitution. The close connection between mental and physical health was recognized. Mental illness in its early stages was treated both by a kind of amateur psychoanalysis—advising the patient to avoid solitude and idleness, encouraging him to keep calm, playing him music—and by such purely physical remedies as change of diet and frequent exercise. Because medicine was so much more a matter of theory than of practice—the practising surgeon rated lower on the social scale than the theoretical physician—many educated men were their own doctors. Milton certainly believed that a proper education should include the rudiments of medical theory, and he is thought to have made his own health worse by amateur remedies. It is possible, however, that expert medical attention would have been no better for him. Despite great advances in research and surgical technique in the seventeenth century, practice lagged a long way behind theory; bleeding and purging were still the standard remedies for most ailments, and doctors lost many patients because no one yet realized the danger of using unsterilized instruments.

Milton's constant insistence on the importance of temperance in food and drink, which may seem fussy to a modern reader, is easier to understand if one sees it in the context of contemporary theory as to how the digestive process provided the link between body and soul. Basically, the transformation of matter into spirit was explained by analogy with the evaporation of water to form first steam and then air. In the human body, the liquid element was supplied by the four *humours* which were extracted from food in the digestive tract. These were blood, phlegm, green bile (which came from the liver) and black bile (which came from the spleen). When these constantly moving liquids reached the liver, the process of 'concoction', or heating, caused them to evaporate and rise in the form of 'spirits'. They mounted first to the heart and then to the brain, which was generally taken to be the location of the rational soul. As they ascended they became increasingly rarified, so that by the time they reached the brain they were almost completely non-material.

If one of the four humours predominated over the others, the brain would naturally be affected. Since the time of the Greeks, human personalities had been classified on the basis of the humours theory as: 1. *sanguine*—the most satisfactory type, as blood was the most invigorating and beneficient of the humours; 2. *phlegmatic*—most women were thought to belong to this type, whose cold and moist nature was supposed to explain their tendency to tearfulness; 3. *choleric*—also known as bilious, because this type was dominated by the green bile; 4. *melancholic*—the humour most associated with mental illness, though it was the most fashionable in the early seventeenth century because it was thought to accompany exceptional intelligence. The popularity of this classification of the four humours, which long outlasted the medical theory in which it originated, probably had something to do with the neat way in which it linked up with the four elements, the four seasons of the year, the four ages of man, and so on.

The mental and physical health of a man, then, depended on his maintaining a proper balance of humours and hence an adequate supply of spirits to the brain. It was the spirits which enabled the soul to control the body; if a man was listless and unable to act, he was said to be 'out of spirits'. It could thus be shown that two such apparently different entities as soul and body might yet influence each other through the action of intermediate substances.

How far the soul and body were actually separate was one of the chief subjects of speculation in Milton's time. This was partly because of the interest which the Renaissance took in Plato's writings. According to Plato, the soul was immortal and completely independent of the body; not only did it live after the body's death, but it had also lived before its birth. The body was only its temporary prison. Plato went on to draw further consequences which most Christians were unwilling to accept. If the soul could leave one body, it could also enter another. Plato suggested that each soul had many lives in which it made itself worthy of heaven, and that each successive life was a reward or punishment for the way in which the previous one had been lived. Some of the early Christian fathers took up this idea. Indeed, Origen (third century A.D.) believed that, after a series of reincarnations, all souls, including those of Satan and his angels, would be saved at last. But his views were condemned as heretical in A.D. 400. The doctrine of reincarnation detracted from the importance of any individual life, since it gave the sinner more chances than one on the earth. Thus, although English poets found it an attractive idea to play around with, they could not take it altogether seriously. There was a further side effect of Platonism, which Milton also disapproved of. By relegating the body to the position of a prison to the soul, it encouraged an attitude of extreme asceticism, shame and contempt for the physical side of life. Though Milton has a great deal to say about the importance of temperance, he also ridicules the folly of those who think that there is anything inherently virtuous in mortifying the flesh. Temperance is *not* total abstinence, though some modern uses of the word tend to confuse the two.

Milton's view was that all matter was created by God and was therefore good. The difference between earth and heaven, like the difference between man and angels, was one of degree not of kind. He seems even to have half accepted the Platonic belief in 'middle spirits', 'Betwixt the angelical and human kind' (*PL* III.462), who, like the Attendant Spirit in *Comus*, might inhabit the moon, the intersection between the mortal and immortal worlds. Human beings became more angel-like as their souls and bodies became more refined, but the soul did not leave the body, from which it was inseparable. Milton was in fact a 'mortalist'—that is, he believed that the soul died with the body and revived only at the resurrection. To believe that the soul was created immortal was, he thought, to deny the need for the resurrection and to open the way for such superstitions as Purgatory, prayers for the dead, and ghosts.

Because he believed that the soul was matter Milton has been called a materialist, but it would be equally accurate to describe him as a spiritualist, since he also believed that the body was spirit, a 'living soul'. He envisaged a dynamic universe in which everything was constantly aspiring upward towards its Creator. The body transformed its food into spirit, man's virtuous life drew him closer and closer to the angels, and the angels grew more and more purely spiritual as they approached nearer to God. Raphael explains to Adam that

> of elements
> The grosser feeds the purer, earth the sea,
> Earth and the sea feed air, the air those fires
> Ethereal, and as lowest first the moon. . . .
> Nor doth the moon no nourishment exhale
> From her moist continent to higher orbs.
> The sun that light imparts to all, receives
> From all his alimental recompense
> In humid exhalations, and at even
> Sups with the ocean
>
> (*PL* V. 415–26).

And he proves his own material nature by taking lunch with the couple. If Adam and Eve remain obedient, he tells them,

> Your bodies may at last turn all to Spirit,
> Improved by tract of time, and winged ascend
> Ethereal, as we, or may at choice
> Here or in heavenly Paradises dwell
>
> (V, 497–500).

The downward motion takes place as the result of sin. Both the rebel angels and the first human beings are dragged literally downwards, into hell or into their graves in the earth. Moloch knows, when he urges the other angels to make an assault on heaven,

> That in our proper motion we ascend
> Up to our native seat: descent and fall
> To us is adverse
>
> (II, 75–7).

But he does not see the irony in his words. The natural motion of all living things is towards God, but by turning away from him the evil angels have made it impossible for themselves to reascend. Even so, they succeed after the fall of Man in becoming princes of the middle region of the air, where we find them in *Paradise Regained*.

In the life of man, the upward motion was that of Reason and the downward one that of Passion. Milton, following the Aristotelean tradition, explained the process of human action by a threefold hierarchy of Reason, Will, and Passion. Ideally, Reason saw what needed to be done, Will received directions from Reason and carried them out, and Passion responded emotionally or instinctively to the situation. If the Will took its directions from Passion instead of Reason, disaster would result, not because Passion was necessarily wrong in its advice, but because it was necessary for Reason and Passion to work together. The happy man was one whose desires were not at war with his moral sense. We nowadays tend to equate passion with energy. But the word 'passion' comes from the same root as 'passive'. To be passionate is not to act but to be acted upon. Christ's Passion was his suffering and death on the cross.

Milton often uses food as a symbol of temptation because it is both good in itself and a possible object of abuse. The magic cup of Comus, the apple on the tree of knowledge, the banquet offered to Christ by Satan, and perhaps even the feast of the Philistines to which Samson is invited, are all designed to appeal to Passion, for which another word is Appetite. It is only by exercising his reason that the hero can know whether or not to follow his natural instinct and accept the offer. Thus the Lady refuses Comus's cup, as Christ refuses Satan's banquet, because the offer comes from an evil source and therefore cannot be good. Eve succumbs to Satan's temptation because she fails to see that his apparently plausible and rational arguments go against the highest command of Reason, which is to love and obey God. The case of Samson is more complicated, because his reason, unlike that of the other three characters, is clouded by sin. His instinctive reaction, which Reason seems to confirm, is to refuse to go to the banquet; it is only God's special grace which reveals to him that he is permitted to make use of apparent evil to accomplish a greater good. God's chosen hero is above all laws, and in a fallen world man can no longer rely entirely on his reason. 'Down Reason, then,' sing the Chorus, but they add, 'at least vain reasonings down' (l. 322). There are good temptations as well as evil ones.

All this emphasis on the role of Reason makes the modern reader want to ask, 'What about the unconscious mind?' Milton's views on this are those of his period. It was generally believed that dreams, stray fantasies, and sudden irrational impulses might be explained either as the influence of God or the devil or as the workings of Fancy without Reason's control. Many Puritans, notably John Bunyan, went through agonies of self-doubt because they held themselves responsible for every lurid fantasy that their over-introspective minds turned up. The hero of *Pilgrim's Progress*, journeying through the Valley of the Shadow of Death, is tormented by devils whispering horrible blasphemies which he imagines to be his own thoughts. In the same way, Eve, describing her dream to Adam in Book V of *Paradise Lost*, is frightened that she has somehow done something wrong by dreaming of a sinful action. Adam does not know that the dream was really sent by Satan, nor does he recognize the sexual symbolism of flying, which has fascinated modern commentators, but he comforts his wife by explaining it in terms of their conversation on the previous evening: they had been talking about the tree of knowledge, so it was natural enough that she should dream of eating its fruit. It is not a sin for her to do so:

> Evil into the mind of god or man
> May come and go, so unapproved, and leave
> No spot or blame behind
>
> (V. 117–19).

In other words, only the thoughts of the conscious mind can be sinful, because these have been admitted by Reason. Though Milton's view has nothing in common with the modern tendency to exalt the unconscious as being more 'real' than the conscious mind, it is not repressive. Human emotions were not, any more than the human body, something to be ashamed of; rather, they had to be kept in good order by Reason. No emotional impulse was either good or bad in itself. Milton recognizes, for instance, the possibility of both a righteous anger and an unrighteous love: the one he expressed in his political pamphlets and in characters like Abdiel and Samson, the other in his treatment of Adam's fall and the love of Samson and Dalila.

The fact that all human emotions might be used as a force for good allowed Milton to stress the value of individualism in personality as much as of noncomformity in religion. *L'Allegro* and *Il Penseroso* are the highest types of sanguine and melancholy temperaments respectively, showing that neither is incompatible with innocence and happiness. 'No man', he declared in his *Apology for Smectymnuus*, is 'forced wholly to dissolve that groundwork of nature which God created in him, the sanguine to empty out all his sociable liveliness, the choleric to expel quite the unsinning predominance of his anger.' God intended 'that each radical humour and passion, wrought upon and corrected as it ought, might be made the proper mold and foundation of every man's peculiar gifts and virtues'. All scientific theory, for Milton, came back in the end to religion. As we shall see, the same was also true of his political views.

3 Political and religious background

Charles I and Laud

Milton spent a good part of his time between 1649 and 1655 in saying that Charles I had been incompetent, wicked and tyrannical. The first of these was certainly true. The King was not a good politician. His real interests were in the arts (he was an enthusiastic collector, a good dancer, and a fine musician) and in his family. He had led a rather sheltered childhood because of poor health and did not become heir to the throne until he was twelve; up to that time, he had been overshadowed by his more popular and gifted elder brother Prince Henry. As a result his natural timidity, which cut him off from close knowledge of his subjects, also led him to rely too much on the advice of others. And unfortunately he was given a great deal of it, mostly contradictory.

He did not, however, hold a tyrannical theory of government. Whoever wrote *Eikon Basilike* was expressing views close to Charles's in declaring that the 'divinest liberty' was 'to will what men should, and to do what they so will, according to Reason, Laws, and Religion'. Milton, as we shall see, held basically the same concept of freedom. And Charles would have agreed with what Milton wrote in his *Second Defense* (1654): 'If every good man is a king . . . it follows by the same logic that every bad man is a tyrant, each in his own degree.' Both men felt that the King was responsible to his subjects, as they to him, and could be punished for failing to live up to his responsibility.

Where the King and Milton differed was in their application of these principles to the particular case of Charles himself. Charles believed that he had fulfilled his duties as king and allowed his subjects as much freedom as they were capable of enjoying. This is why, in 1649, he steadfastly refused to acknowledge the right of the House of Commons to put him on trial at all. In Milton's view, and that of the men who voted for the execution, the King had broken his contract with his subjects by making war on them and by his vacillating, or, as they saw it, treacherous, behaviour in the negotiations which followed.

The King's execution was an unexpected outcome of the Civil War, and was not thought of, much less desired, by anyone before 1648. Both Houses of Parliament had frequently protested about his attempts at reigning alone and raising funds without consulting them (particularly between 1629 and 1640), but many of the protesters nevertheless fought on his side during the war. As for Milton, he showed no sign of hostility to the royal prerogative until much later; what interested him was the religious freedom without which mere political freedom could not exist. Similarly, it was on a religious issue—whether Episcopal church government and the

Prayer Book should be foisted on the Scots—that Parliament and popular sympathy first united against the King.

This Scottish campaign, which took place while Milton was on his way home from the continent in 1639, was the culmination of the Church policy of Charles and Archbishop William Laud, whose aim had always been to identify loyalty to the King with loyalty to the State Church. Laud used the Church to support the state, as when, in 1640, each parish priest was directed to read out, four times a year, a sentence affirming that kingship was 'the ordinance of God himself, founded in the prime laws of nature'. He also used the state to support the Church: bishops held more secular posts than at any time since the Reformation and were responsible for the censorship of all writings. This concentration of power in ecclesiastical hands completely reversed the Reformation subordination of Church to state and caused widespread fears of a return to popery.

Yet what Laud actually wanted to accomplish was a reform of the Anglican Church from within. He was not a cruel man, and his reforms could not be described as a persecution. Nevertheless their intention and effect was to freeze out of the Church all but one of the many different kinds of Protestantism which had previously been coexisting within it. We have seen that Milton felt himself 'church-outed' by these measures. Before Laud set to work, a graduate in divinity who found himself unable to accept all the Thirty-nine Articles might still be allowed to preach as a 'lecturer' who was not attached to a particular church, or he might be employed as a private chaplain. Country gentlemen of Puritan sympathies banded together to buy up vacant livings and fill them with preachers of their own choice. Laud put a stop to these practices and thus succeeded in alienating not only Puritan but much orthodox opinion, for these gentlemen, whatever their beliefs, deeply resented his highhanded interference with their privileges. And Laud's unpopularity rebounded on Charles I.

The Archbishop shared with his artistic King a keen interest in building and restoring churches, which he adorned with stained glass, statuary, and religious paintings such as had not been seen there since the Reformation. Charles personally paid for the construction of a new portico to St Paul's cathedral, not only because the old West front needed restoring but also because, in the interest of preserving the dignity of the House of God, people were to be encouraged to meet and talk in the portico rather than, as had been the custom, in the cathedral itself. Like the church building (and, in fact, like Charles's court), the church service was also to be dignified and beautiful, with emphasis on the element of ritual and ceremony rather than preaching.

Yet Puritans would walk miles to hear a sermon several hours long, and during the Civil War Cromwell's soldiers stabled their horses in the cathedral which Charles and Laud had helped to restore. It is not surprising that High Church men thought of their enemies as ignorant fanatics. The odd thing is that hostility to the Laudian type of church service was not confined to insensitive bigots. In 1641 Bishop Joseph Hall, bewildered by the attitude of the reformers, asked them point-blank, 'Tell me, is this liturgy good or evil?' It was Milton himself who in his line-by-line *Animadversions* on Hall's pamphlet, replied, 'It is evil'. To understand how a man of his intelligence and sensitivity could feel this way, we need to look more closely at the nature of Puritanism.

Presbyterians and Independents

In spirit, if not in name, Puritanism really preceded the Reformation. Christianity has known many revivalist movements, all designed to restore the original simplicity of religion as it is described in the Gospels. When the name first came into circulation in the Elizabethan period, a Puritan might be any Protestant who felt that his church had not gone far enough in dissociating itself from Rome. Many Elizabethans had Puritan leanings—Milton's favourite poet, Spenser, for instance, and Sir Philip Sidney, who died fighting for the Protestant cause in the Netherlands. Others were called Puritans by their enemies, for the word was used very loosely. Some Puritan views were widespread even among Charles's followers at the start of the Civil War. There were 'Puritan' bishops too. But Spenser, Sidney, and their later counterparts did not leave the Church of England; they believed in working from within for reform.

Most Puritans were basically Calvinist in their theology: that is, they believed in some sort of predestination. This did not make them fatalistic in their attitude toward life. On the contrary, they worked the more vigorously as they identified themselves with the purposes of God and believed that their prosperity was a sign of his favour. Practicality was a keynote of Puritanism. Impatient of metaphysics and mysticism, Puritan ministers went in for plain, direct sermons and the portions of the Bible in which they took most interest were those which dealt with the struggles of the individual soul for salvation. They became experts on the psychology of sin and the wiles of Satan, who was very real to them: 'He pulled and I pulled,' wrote Bunyan in *Grace Abounding* (1666), 'but, God be praised, I got the better of him.'

They saw Satan at work in the actions of their enemies. The Anglican liturgy was 'evil', because it denied them the right to speak to God in their own words. Even the Lord's Prayer, however beautiful, lost its value if it became only words that everyone mumbled by rote. Perhaps they were also aware that one reason Laud wanted to prohibit long sermons was that, having himself used the pulpit for government propaganda, he was afraid of its being used against him. The sermon, particularly during the period of strict press censorship, was one of the most effective means of disseminating anti-government views.

The Presbyterians were distinguished from other left wing opponents of Laud's Anglicanism by their belief that episcopal church government ought to be replaced by that of a Synod of Presbyters, or Elders, on both a local and national level. This was the system that already prevailed in Scotland. During the three years leading up to the Civil War (1639–42), Charles's inept Scottish policy created a great deal of sympathy with Presbyterianism and encouraged English Prebyterians to declare themselves. Thus, when the war first broke out, most of the men on the Parliamentary side assumed that it would be brief and that its outcome would be the restoration of Charles I at the head of a Presbyterian state church similar to the one in Scotland. The Scots themselves, entering the war on the side of Parliament in 1643, made it a condition of their support that all Englishmen should take the Solemn League and Covenant to defend Presbyterianism. Through the efforts of Sir Henry Vane ('young in years but in sage counsel old', as Milton later described him in a sonnet), the Covenant was reworded in such a way as to make it possible for men to sign it without committing themselves to Presbyterian rule.

For already it was becoming apparent that the Scottish system would not work in England. Once episcopacy had been abolished, there was no longer any common cause to unite Presbyterians with other Protestant sects; they had known what they did not want, but not what to put in its place. The Presbyterians, though they may have looked like revolutionaries to Laud, were basically middle-class moderates who disliked their rival religious sects much more than they had disliked the Anglican Church. They soon started to behave just like the bishops against whom they had been rebelling, and Milton eventually concluded (in a satiric sonnet of 1646) that 'New Presbyter is but Old Priest writ large'.

The reimposition of licensing in 1643, against which Milton wrote his *Areopagitica*, is a good example of the way in which the revolution failed to live up to the hopes of some of its partisans. Milton seems to have felt that freedom of the press had been one of the original aims of the Long Parliament. But in fact it was only an accident that there was no press censorship between 1641 and 1643. By a practice that had existed since Elizabeth's time, the licensing and printing of books was under the control of the Star Chamber—a high court of justice responsible only to the crown—and the Company of Stationers, which had a monopoly on printing and hence a vested interest in the suppression of illegal rivals. When the Star Chamber was abolished in 1641, there was a temporary breakdown of the licensing machinery. This was inconvenient for the Stationers' Company, because it allowed a number of small unofficial presses to spring up and threaten their monopoly. They therefore presented a petition to Parliament in 1643, asking for the re-establishment of licensing. Many members of Parliament had already been demanding the same thing; they were genuinely horrified at the amount of unorthodox literature that was pouring out of the press. They duly passed, in June of the same year, a Licensing Order which was basically a continuation of the system that had been in operation under Charles I. Nothing was supposed to be printed that had not first received the approval of an official licenser; it must have the author's and printer's names on the titlepage; it could only be printed at one of a restricted number of presses belonging to the Stationers' Company. Disobedience was punishable by imprisonment.

In practice the Order was not obeyed. Milton published all but one of his divorce pamphlets without a licence, though with his initials on the titlepage. *Areopagitica*, of course, was unlicensed; it also carried his full name. Despite objections from some members of Parliament, Milton got away with this defiance, and his case seems to have been typical. Nevertheless it marks his break with the Presbyterians. Moreover his main argument in *Areopagitica*, that diverse opinions must be allowed to fight it out in public, and that the conflict could do nothing but good, went along with a belief in religious toleration and a distrust of 'obedient unanimity' (as he contemptuously called it) that was soon to put him in the camp of the Presbyterians' chief opponents, the Independents.

Opposition of Presbyterian to Independent was not necessarily doctrinal; many Independents held orthodox Calvinist views. Where they differed from the Presbyterians was in their denial of the need for any established church. Their demand for religious toleration grew out of an awareness that the very number and smallness of Protestant sects required them to coexist whether they liked it or not. It was these Independents who made up most of Cromwell's New Model Army, and the second phase of the Civil War, after the defeat of the Royalists in 1645, was the conflict between them and the mainly Presbyterian Parliament which, by continuing to advocate a state church, and by negotiating with Charles I, seemed to them to be betraying its own defenders. They defeated the Presbyterian army at Preston in 1648, took control of Parliament, and, against the wishes of many of their own members, presided over the trial and execution of Charles I. These men, who wanted no church or minister to come between them and their consciences, were the most original and forward-looking thinkers of their day, but they were very few in number. Their ascendancy represents the final stage in the process whereby Parliament became divorced from popular feeling. One proof of this is that the Commonwealth did not feel able to repeal the Licensing Order, even though illegally printed Royalist pamphlets continued to make it look ridiculous. By agreeing to act as Licenser, though he performed the task with much greater tolerance than was shown under either Laud or the Presbyterians, Milton tacitly accepted the fact that the Commonwealth was not founded on popular consent.

The revolution failed, essentially, because the revolutionary governments, having fought against what they regarded as tyranny, first Anglican, then Presbyterian, found themselves in a position where they had either to become tyrants themselves or let the country fall into a state of anarchy. This dilemma was first seen when it became apparent that the only alternatives to Anglicanism were a Presbyterian state church or no state church at all. Milton's sonnets to Cromwell and Vane in 1652 advised them to choose the latter. He praised Vane for respecting the bounds between civil and religious authority and urged Cromwell to 'save free Conscience from the paw of hireling wolves'—that is, a clergy paid by the state. It was no use; a state church was set up, though one which allowed more freedom to dissenters than had hitherto been known.

Cromwell attempted to run the country on the basis of solidarity with all Protestants at home or abroad. When, in 1655, the Protestant Vaudois were massacred in Piedmont (the incident which gave rise to Milton's sonnet, discussed on p. 132), Cromwell showed that England was prepared to defend the interests of even the smallest Protestant community. In letters drafted by Milton, the leaders of all the Protestant nations in Europe were called on to join in condemnation of the massacre, for, he wrote, 'the protestant name and cause, although they differ among themselves in some things of little consequence, is nevertheless the same in general, and united in one common interest'. But the government was unable to create the same sense of a common interest in England itself.

Religious intolerance was based on more than fear of the multiplication of eccentric religions; it went along with a fear of the breakdown of law and order, property, and the class structure. It is easy to see how the radical sects could also become radical in their political and social views. Because they believed that it required no special learning to read Scripture rightly and that the poorest and most ignorant man might have more of 'the Spirit' in him than the scholar or clergyman, they saw no need for a separation of clergy from laity. Many Puritans felt, like Milton, that it was wrong to require the congregation to pay tithes for the support of a minister who ought to be earning his living like the rest of them.

Yet few men actually took the crucial step from believing in the spiritual equality of all men before God to demanding their political and social equality in this life. Milton certainly did not; his *Christian Doctrine* warns almsgivers against 'the absurdity of equalizing those whom nature never intended for an equality'. The two genuinely radical groups of the period, the Levellers and the Diggers, were disowned by Presbyterian and Independent alike.

The Levellers were the larger and more influential movement, drawing much of their support from the army. Their most eloquent spokesman, John Lilburne, was an admirer of Milton's political writings; Milton does not seem to have returned the admiration. At the height of their power, in 1647–8, they proposed a new con-

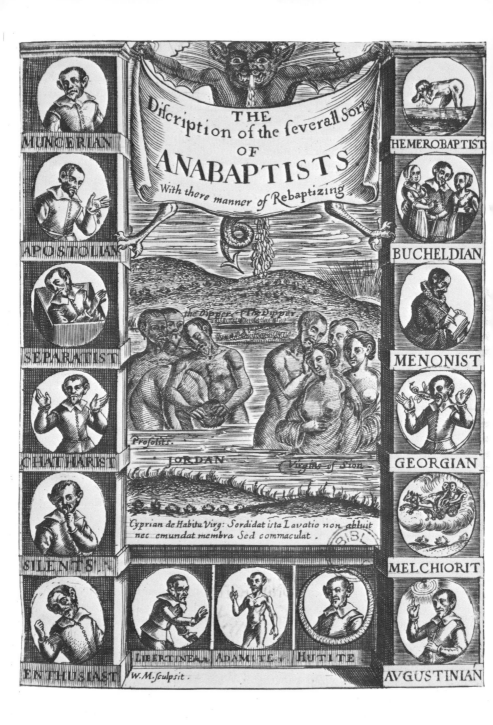

Title page of Daniel Featley, *The Dippers Dipt, 1645*

stitution for the country, called for regular meetings of the House of Commons, which was to be the supreme law of the land, and for an extended though not universal franchise. The Diggers were more radical. Their leader, Gerrard Winstanley, who declared that 'Jesus Christ is the head Leveller', had derived a communist theory of land ownership from his study of the Scriptures. To dramatize their convictions, he and his followers began communal cultivation of a patch of ground near London in April of 1649. But the newly established Commonwealth government turned against both Levellers and Diggers, though some of its leaders had been sympathetic to them before their rise to power. Lilburne spent most of the rest of his life in exile or prison and the Digger movement petered out about a year after its beginning.

There were two reasons why Puritans, except in these isolated cases, never became wholly democratic. The first was that most of them were moderately well-off or selfmade men. The self-righteousness to which they were liable in religious matters tended, in the economic sphere, to take the form of contempt for the 'undeserving poor', who must, they thought, be either idle or wicked. The second was that many of them believed the Millennium to be close at hand —the thousand-year reign of Christ on earth with his saints, which the Bible seemed to prophesy for the year 1666; such a prospect naturally made all earthly, manmade utopias fade into irrelevance. In the end, the promised year brought, not the descent of Christ in his glory, but the Great Fire of London. Much of the apathy and cynicism of Restoration society may perhaps be attributed to the failure of this great hope.

The Commonwealth leaders, then, were much more conservative than Milton in their attitude to religious conformity, and much too frightened of economic and political revolution to support the Levellers and Diggers. In other words, they lost their former supporters on the left wing without winning any new ones on the right: a common cause of the fall of revolutionary governments. In 1660 men restored both Charles II and the Church of England because, when it came to the point, they feared authoritarianism less than anarchy. Restoration England responded to twenty years of 'enthusiasm' (its name for religious fanaticism) by becoming sceptical of all political and religious idealists. It came to be felt that men ought either to accept the state and Church into which they were born or else keep quiet about their disagreement. This was a long-lasting attitude: in 1734, Jonathan Richardson, a great admirer of Milton's, prefaced his comments on the political writings by saying, 'Let us now consider him whether in the right or not; that point is settled by our superiors'. What Milton and other Puritans had tried to say, nearly a hundred years before, was that 'our superiors' have no right to make up our minds for us.

Milton and religion

At the beginning of his literary career, Milton was a fairly orthodox Anglican: St Peter in *Lycidas* actually wears a bishop's mitre. By the end of his life, he attended no church at all and did not even hold family prayers in his home. This movement from centre to extreme left was paralleled by his political development and is typical of what happened to a good many people during the 1640s and 50s. For example, there were those who called themselves Seekers because, in search of the true religion, they went from church to church and found none to satisfy them. Milton did not make this kind of search. Having decided early on that the Christian owed his spiritual allegiance to God alone, he wasted no time exploring the claims of rival sects, though he advocated tolerance for all except Roman Catholics. He was too much of an individualist to find a home in any organized religious group.

The particular type of Anglicanism in which he grew up had a strongly Calvinist flavour, and Calvinism formed the basis of his later religious belief. But it was a less harsh belief than Calvin's original doctrine of predestination, and was in fact the object of attack by strict Presbyterians. In the modified view of the Dutch theologian Arminius, men were predestined only in a conditional sense: that is, God predestined the good to salvation and the bad to damnation, but he did not ordain that the one group should be good and the other bad. Hence man had free will after all. It is this Arminian view that God states in Book III of *Paradise Lost*. His distinction between foreknowledge and predestination—

> if I foreknew,
> Foreknowledge had no influence on their fault,
> Which had no less proved certain unforeknown
> (III. 117–19).

—goes back to St. Augustine, who explains the apparent contradiction between God's foreknowledge and man's free will by the fact that all time, for God, exists in an eternal present. God sees future events as if they were happening now, but does not cause them to happen, any more than a human being who foresaw them could be said to be their cause.

Milton was never, then, a strict Calvinist. But Calvinism was a way of life as well as a religious doctrine, and Milton was one of many Puritans who, although they distrusted the Presbyterian form of church government, nevertheless retained many of its basic attitudes. His *Christian Doctrine*, which represents the point his religious thought had reached by the end of the Commonwealth period, is both Puritan and Calvinist in its insistence on the superiority of Scripture over tradition, and of the individual conscience over even Scripture. The essentially practical nature of its advice is also characteristic. He recommends the domestic virtues of frugality and industry, finds nothing wrong in the desire to get on in the world, and distinguishes between virtue and fanaticism. We are forbidden to lie to our neighbour, he points out, but are under no obligation to speak truth to our enemy, especially when we have not been asked for it and when it would be suicidal to do so. It is hard to realize that the author of this coolly sensible advice is the same man who was writing fervent Republican tracts up to the eve of the Restoration.

This practical approach to religion is also shown in Milton's frequent statement that it is pointless to speculate about theological mysteries which are of no help to us in leading our lives. The doctrine of the Trinity is an example of the sort of mystical concept which Milton generally disliked, though *The Christian Doctrine* is the only place where he specifically denies it. He believes that the Son was created by the Father, rather than co-eternal with him, and is consequently a separate being. How, he asks, could Christ be an intercessor between man and God, if he was identical with God? As for the Holy Spirit, Milton feels that it is probably of a somewhat lower order than Father and Son, but that in any case its precise nature cannot be a vital article of faith, since so little is said about it in the Scriptures. Throughout *Paradise Lost*, the Son and the Spirit are represented as agents of the Father, who is the essence and source of all their actions. Both the Son's casting out of the rebel angels and his volunteering to sacrifice himself for man are more dramatic if seen in this light. The Son is omnipotent only by virtue of his faith in his Father and he has to prove, by his actions, that he alone is worthy to be Son of God. In *Paradise Regained*, moreover, Christ is shown to be human rather than divine (Milton does not believe that he could have been both at once), and consequently unsure of his identity. The temptation in the wilderness would have no interest if Christ were not human enough to be tempted.

This denial of the Trinity is the chief of Milton's famous 'heresies'; the technical name for it is Arianism or Subordinationism. But it is important to note that theological speculation in the seventeenth century had touched on doctrines far more exotic than Milton's— for instance, reincarnation, the denial that hell was eternal, belief that the end of the world was at hand. Religious writers dabbled in Oriental religions, Jewish mysticism, pagan philosophy, and the study of those Church fathers who had been called heretics by a later age. Compared with these, Milton's mild eccentricities, such as his defence of polygamy in some circumstances and his anti-sabbatarianism, are hardly noticeable. They may be seen, like his Arianism and his exposition of the Puritan ethic generally, as a result of that ostentatiously logical, practical attitude to life which is frequently found in the most idealistic and impractical of men.

When he comes to advise his readers how to approach the Scriptures, Milton again takes a practical, almost Fundamentalist, point of view. He knew the allegorical tradition of scriptural interpretation, which had been applied to the Old Testament since before the time of Christ; it is possible that at least one such tradition, the view that the Garden of Eden represented the Soul of Man, with Adam as Reason and Eve as Passion, is reflected in the imagery of *Paradise Lost*. But on the whole he felt obliged to reject allegorical interpretation because it left Scripture open to any fanciful ideas that one cared to read into it. Near the beginning of *The Christian Doctrine* he advises his readers to take Scripture literally, since, though we cannot know God as he really is, the Bible at least shows us how he wishes us to conceive of him. Similarly, in *Paradise Lost*, he is not afraid to describe divine personages in human terms. Though he frequently reminds us, as Raphael also reminds Adam, that the reality is far beyond anything we can imagine, he also wants us to identify ourselves with the heroes of these stories, which is not likely to happen if we think of them only as symbolic figures.

Still, Milton had read the Church Fathers and many other biblical commentators, and his epics were bound to take some of their views into account. After all, the Genesis story of Adam and Eve is extremely brief, while the story of Satan is the result of the linking by commentators of a number of separate scriptural passages: the serpent in Genesis, the fallen star ('O Lucifer, son of the morning') of Isaiah's prophecy, the 'adversary' of the New Testament, and, from The Revelation, 'the dragon, that old serpent, which is the Devil, and Satan' (20:2). This linking-up process, which began with pre-Christian Rabbinical writers, was taken still further after the time of Christ, notably by St Paul, who interpreted the Old Testament as a series of prophecies or symbols of the Christian story. The fall of man, relatively unimportant in the context of the Old Testament, became the crucial event of human history, the source of all our sins, the crime which Christ's sacrifice had to expiate. Other Old Testament figures were also seen as foreshadowing Christ: Isaac (whose father Abraham was told by God to sacrifice him), Joshua (who led his people into the Promised Land), Jonah (because the three days he spent in the belly of the whale were taken to prefigure Christ's death and resurrection), and Samson (because he freed his people by his death).

But it was Adam above all who was compared with Christ, as Eve with the Virgin Mary. Parallels were found between the Tree of Knowledge which made man mortal and the cross which redeemed him; in one tradition, the cross was supposed to have been made of the wood of that tree, in another, to have been erected on the same spot where the tree had grown. It was held that Christ, the second Adam, had to live through a perfected version of the first Adam's life in order fully to atone for the original sin. Thus Adam's eating of the apple was contrasted with Christ's refusal, when tempted by the devil, to turn stones into bread. St Paul carefully draws the parallel: 'For as by Man came death, so also by Man came the resurrection unto life' (1 Corinthians 15:21).

It was St Augustine who, in his *City of God*, fixed the orthodox Christian interpretation of the Biblical events with which Milton deals in his epics. He identified the serpent in the Garden of Eden with the devil and, because all God's creations must originally have been created good, he concluded that Satan and his followers were angels who had fallen from their original perfection. Accepting to some extent the allegorical reading of the fall, he took the forbidden fruit as a symbol of obedience and, following St Paul, distinguished between Adam's sin (committed in full knowledge) and Eve's (the result of ignorance). He maintained that sexual relations between man and woman had existed before the fall and were not, as others had argued, a consequence of it; thus, sex was inherently good. Augustine's distinction between fallen and unfallen sexuality is the basis of Milton's.

As the Bible gives no definite explanation of the fall of the angels, several hypotheses had been offered to account for it. In one version, Satan was cast out from heaven *after* he tempted Adam and Eve. Another version, found in one of the apocryphal books of the Bible, makes him Eve's seducer, and Milton seems to have had this tradition in mind when he gave Satan the style of a courtly lover in his speeches to Eve. But the main cause of Satan's downfall was usually taken to be pride, which was thus regarded as the chief of the deadly sins. Passages in which Isaiah and Ezekiel prophesied the fall of the king of Babylon were interpreted as an account of the fall of Satan:

> For thou hast said in thy heart, I will ascend into heaven, I will exalt my throne above the stars of God . . . I will ascend above the heights of the clouds: I will be like the Most High
>
> (Isaiah 14:13–14).

> Thine heart was lifted up because of thy beauty: thou hast corrupted thy wisdom by reason of thy brightness
>
> (Ezekiel 28:17).

So the chief of the damned spirits was believed to have been a bright angel who, dazzled by his own splendour, tried to usurp the place of God and was punished by being cast down into hell. Such was the traditional portrayal of the devil in, for instance, medieval drama, though after his fall he tends to become a grotesque and even comic character, swearing, letting off fireworks, and generally behaving like a monster in a horror film.

Genesis does not say when the angels fell, and Milton's decision to make the war in heaven precede the creation of the world is to some extent a departure from tradition. St Augustine had suggested that perhaps the fall of the angels was meant to be implied in the phrase about God's dividing the light from the darkness on the first day of Creation. He noted that, although the Bible declares that God saw that the light was good, night and darkness are not so described. The separation of good from evil, like that of light from darkness, seemed to him proof that God intended the beauty of the world to arise from the constant opposition of contrary principles, like 'an exquisite poem set off with antitheses'. The implication that the angels fell virtually as soon as they were created smacked too much of predestination to satisfy Milton. By making the creation of the world an answer to Satan's destructive action in warring on God, he was able to emphasize instead the rhythm of divine providence, whereby each Satanic attempt at destruction is followed by a still more wonderful display of God's creative energy.

But Augustine's appreciation of the poetic effect produced by the light–dark contrast is very much in the spirit of Milton's work. Even before his blindness the poet saw the world, both physically and morally, as black and white. His political extremism, his impatience of all attempts of Church and state to impose compromise and moderation on the free spirit, have their literary counterparts in the imagery of contrast which he uses: the snow-covered world and 'bright-harnessed angels' of the *Nativity Ode* are set against the 'twilight shade' and 'temples dim' of the defeated pagan gods; the dark wood of *Comus* is brightened by 'the sun-clad power of chastity'. Yet, like Augustine again, Milton avoids the heresy of making the evil, dark principle as powerful as the good one. The darkness contains some reflection of the sun and is never altogether able to black out the light.

Milton's concept of freedom

When the members of the Long Parliament had been sitting for only a short time, Milton wrote that they were superior to the heroes who had been celebrated in the literature of Greece and Rome, 'for those ancient worthies delivered men from such tyrants as were content to enforce only an outward obedience, letting the mind be as free as it could, but these have freed us from a doctrine of tyranny, that offered violence and corruption even to the inward persuasion' (*Apology for Smectymnuus*). They looked very different to him when he wrote, in a digression in his *History of Britain* (1670):

> Thus they who but of late were extolled as great deliverers, and had a people wholly at their devotion, by so discharging their trust as we see, did not only weaken and unfit themselves to be dispensers of what liberty they pretended, but unfitted also the people, now grown worse and more disordinate, to receive or to digest any liberty at all. . . . For liberty hath a sharp and double

edge fit only to be handled by just and virtuous men, to bad and dissolute it becomes a mischief unwieldy in their own hands.*

His prose writings bear witness to the whole story of how freedom was won and lost in England, from the enthusiasm of the early pamphlets to the melancholy of *A Ready and Easy Way* (1660), where he felt he was speaking 'the last words of our expiring liberty'.

The theme of freedom also runs through Milton's poetic works from the beginning. The two psalms which he chose to translate at the age of fifteen sing the praises of the Lord who freed the Israelites from the tyrant Pharaoh. The infant Christ of the *Nativity Ode* is seen as the overthrower of the usurper Satan and all his followers. Comus and his crew are put to flight by boys aged nine and eleven. The fall of Satan in both *Paradise Lost* and *Paradise Regained* is the result of the same divine power that also works through Samson when he brings down the pillars of the Philistine temple and sets his people free. Even his use of blank verse for *Paradise Lost* seemed to Milton not merely an aesthetic choice but 'an example set, the first in English, of ancient liberty recovered to heroic poem from the troublesome and modern bondage of rhyming'. The phrase 'ancient liberty' is important: despite his pride in being the first to write a blank verse epic in English, Milton is typical of his age in that he looks to the past for a precedent; the Commons also kept claiming that they were only asking for the restoration of old rights, not the establishment of new ones. Similarly, he had already described his divorce pamphlets as a restating of 'the known rules of ancient liberty'. Like Paradise, Liberty has been lost but can be regained.

The struggle for liberty, in Milton's poems, is portrayed in language of rebellion and violence which, taken by itself, might seem to justify those critics who think that Milton unconsciously identified himself with the cause of Satan. But in fact the violence is largely metaphorical. The life of a Christian was traditionally pictured as a battle, but it was within the human soul that Christ and Satan were at war. Even in *Comus*, although the brothers make a daring raid on the enchanter's den, they are not able to free their sister until helped by Sabrina, the martyr of chastity. And the Lady defeats Comus in words before he is defeated in action.

Yet the zest with which the brothers undertake to fight for virtue's cause is part of the essential optimism of Milton's early work, and finds its parallel in his near-idealization of the Parliamentary leaders and his prophecies of a glorious new birth of liberty for England. The excitement of the early 1640s infected him as it did others. But he was too rational a man to be carried away by the military successes of the Parliamentary forces. In 1648 he wrote in a sonnet to General Fairfax,

> For what can war but endless war still breed,
> Till Truth and Right from Violence be freed?

*Suppressed in 1670 edition, possibly at Milton's own request; first published in 1681.

The overthrowing of episcopacy did not lead to true freedom of worship, nor did the victories of Cromwell and Fairfax make men more virtuous. The Puritans tended to be success-worshippers, and to gloat over each indication that God was on their side, but Milton's sonnet to Cromwell in 1652, though it lists his victories at Preston, Dunbar and Worcester, ends by directing the general's attention away from these to the need for religious liberty in the state:

> peace hath her victories
No less renowned than war.

As we have seen, it was because these peacetime victories could not be won that the Commonwealth eventually collapsed. Milton, who had once thought Englishmen the chosen people of God, later blamed the failure on the national character: 'For Britain (to speak a truth not oft spoken) as it is a land fruitful enough of men stout and courageous in war, so is it naturally not over-fertile of men able to govern justly and prudently in peace' (*History of Britain*). It is not surprising, then, that Milton's post-Restoration epics reject the false glamour of 'fabled knights in battles feigned' (*PL* IX. 30–1). Abdiel's real victory over Satan comes when he recognizes and defies the archangel's evil counsel, not when he strikes him down on the battlefield. Michael tells Adam not to expect the defeat of Satan by Christ to take the form of a duel, and *Paradise Regained* treats the temptation as a battle of words only: Christ specifically rejects any thought of establishing his kingdom by force. Milton had earned the right to praise 'the better fortitude of patience and heroic martyrdom' (*PL* IX. 31–2). He had seen enough battles, and practised the art of patience long enough, to know by experience what he had always said on principle: the only true freedom was the freedom of the virtuous individual to do of his own free will what he ought to do anyway.

This concept of freedom was his solution to the problem which, as we have seen, Parliament could not solve: how to prevent freedom from degenerating into anarchy or relapsing into authoritarianism in order to save its institutions. *Comus* shows how closely virtue and liberty were linked for him. 'Thou canst not touch the freedom of my mind With all thy charms,' the Lady tells Comus, and at the end of the masque the Attendant Spirit sums up the moral: 'Love virtue, she alone is free.' Milton frequently distinguishes between true liberty, which only the virtuous man can possess, and *licence*, which is what vicious men mistake for it. Of those who took his divorce pamphlets to be an encouragement to unbridled sensuality, he wrote that they

> bawl for freedom in their senseless mood,
And still revolt when truth would set them free.
Licence they mean when they cry liberty;
For who loves that, must first be wise and good.

Man had to be wise as well as good, because his virtue depended on his ability to make the right choices. Reason, as Milton said in *Areopagitica*, 'is but choosing'. From this it followed that everything which denied man the right to choose for himself must be evil. A man might be 'a heretic in the truth' if he followed a religion, even the right religion, simply out of habit. The good angels voluntarily choose to obey God, just as Eve chooses to obey Adam. There is no element of constraint in this situation, because reason and emotion go together. 'Freely we serve, Because we freely love,' Raphael tells Adam, and Eve's love for her husband is also an act of choice. She is obeying 'God in him', and should cease to obey him if his advice went against what she knew to be God's command. Thus, no one is really subservient to another person's will, but only to God's will as manifested in him. Milton assumes that the love of the angels for God and of Eve for Adam is completely under the control of Reason, which recognizes the goodness and worthiness of the object loved. Adam's love for Eve ceases to be good when she ceases to deserve it.

Milton applies the same doctrine to his own age, with the distinction that man, since the fall, has to rely on the Holy Spirit within him to make up for the weakness of his reason. Samson, as we have seen, is an example of a man in whom the Spirit overrides both reason and human laws. In most situations, though, Milton felt that men ought to find their freedom in a decision to serve those whom they recognize as their natural superiors. He was even prepared to apply this rule in the domestic sphere, in cases where the wife was the naturally superior partner. Needless to say, he did not expect this to be the case very often. In *Eikonoklastes*, he ridiculed the style in which Charles I had spoken of his Queen in *Eikon Basilike*. 'How fit to govern men,' he exclaimed sarcastically, 'undervaluing and aspersing the great council of his kingdom, in comparison of one woman!'

That Charles should be a slave to his own wife is part of Milton's concept of tyranny as man's subjection to his natural inferiors, a subjection which applies as much to the tyrant himself as to his subjects. The classic statement of this position is Abdiel's speech to Satan:

> Unjustly thou deprav'st it with the name
> Of servitude to serve whom God ordains,
> Or nature; God and nature bid the same,
> When he who rules is worthiest, and excels
> Them whom he governs. This is servitude,
> To serve the unwise, or him who hath rebelled
> Against his worthier, as thine now serve thee.
> Thyself not free, but to thyself enthralled
>   (VI. 174–81).

God cannot be a tyrant, as Satan tries to make out, because He is by nature superior to those whom He rules. This is not true of Charles I. Milton makes his position still clearer in Book XII, when Adam is told of Nimrod, the first man to claim power over other men. In making this claim. Nimrod will usurp the place of God and thus

> from rebellion shall derive his name,
> Though of rebellion others he accuse
> (XII. 36–7).

When Adam is shocked at such presumption, Michael tells him that tyranny of man over men is the logical outcome of the Fall, where the natural rule of reason over passion was upset. This first usurpation was the signal for all the others:

> Since thy original lapse, true liberty
> Is lost, which always with right reason dwells
> Twinned, and from her hath no dividual being:
> Reason in man obscured, or not obeyed,
> Immediately inordinate desires
> And upstart passions catch the government
> From reason, and to servitude reduce
> Man till then free. Therefore since he permits
> Within himself unworthy powers to reign
> Over free reason, God in judgment just
> Subjects him from without to violent lords;
> Who oft as undeservedly enthral
> His outward freedom: tyranny must be,
> Though to the tyrant thereby no excuse
> (XII. 83–96).

Similarly, Christ in *Paradise Regained* turns down Satan's proposal for seizing the throne of Tiberius and liberating the Roman Empire from his tyranny:

> What wise and valiant man would seek to free
> These thus degenerate, by themselves enslaved,
> Or could of inward slaves make outward free?
> (*PR* IV. 143–5).

Milton's experiences had thus made him increasingly pessimistic about men's ability ever to be anything but slaves. His greatest work tells how freedom may be regained, but what it actually shows us is how it was lost.

The critic John Toland wrote in 1698 that 'to display the different effects of Liberty and Tyranny is the chief design of . . . *Paradise Lost*'. In particular, the career of Satan is a poignant study of how loss of virtue leads to the perversion of reason and thus to loss of freedom. St Augustine, writing of the fall of man, noted that the punishment for disobedience was disobedience: 'For what else is man's misery but his own disobedience to himself, so that in consequence of his not being willing to do what he could do, he now wills to do what he cannot?' The same is true of Satan. Though he rebels against God in assertion of his freedom, he soon finds that he is not free to do what he knows to be right:

O then at last relent: is there no place
Left for repentance, none for pardon left?
None left but by submission; and that word
Disdain forbids me, and my dread of shame
Among the spirits beneath

(IV. 79–83).

Though Milton's respect for the individual's sense of his own
identity was too strong to allow him to be an existentialist of the
modern kind, what he displays in this speech of Satan's is a perfect
example of what the existentialist philosopher Sartre calls man's
limitation of his own freedom by the concept of 'character'. Satan,
in other words, has become the prisoner of his image; it is Disdain,
not God, that forbids him to repent. Similarly, Adam and Eve in
the last part of Book IX seem about to turn into the stereotyped
grumbling husband and nagging wife of comedy:

Would thou hadst hearkened to my words, and stayed
With me, as I besought thee, when that strange
Desire of wandering this unhappy morn,
I know not whence possessed thee

(IX. 1134–7).

Was I to have never parted from thy side?
As good have grown there still a lifeless rib

(IX. 1153–4).

It is no wonder that, as critics have been saying for centuries, evil
characters tend to be so much more vividly realized than good ones.
Adam and Eve, like Satan, find themselves trapped by their own
past actions, constantly looking back to them, and unable, like the
good man, to make a free decision at each moment, guided only by
reason.

Readers of Milton sometimes object that his good characters find
it too easy to make the right decisions, because their reason and
passion are so completely in harmony. But the most important
decisions in Milton's works are those which have to be made not by
his characters but by the reader himself. Many critics of Milton, like
many historians of the Civil War, seem to repeat, if in rather subtler
terms, the famous *1066 and All That* division of the *dramatis personae*
into Cavaliers ('Wrong but Wromantic') and Roundheads ('Right
but Repulsive'). Milton is notoriously good at playing devil's
advocate. The lush enticements of Comus, the fine heroic speeches
of Satan in *Paradise Lost* and his even more moving weariness and
despair in *Paradise Regained*, Dalila's smooth justification of her
treachery towards Samson—all these may be designed to enhance
our admiration for the characters who successfully resist such
temptations, but they also force us to make a choice between good
and evil and to recognize that this choice is much harder for us
than for Milton's heroes.

4 Literary background

Some foreign influences

In that passage of his *History of Britain* where he explains the failure of the Commonwealth, Milton makes this interesting comment on the national character:

> The sun, which we want, ripens wits as well as fruits; and as wine and oil are imported to us from abroad, so must ripe understanding and many civil virtues be imported into our minds from foreign writings and examples of best ages: we shall else miscarry still and come short in the attempt of any great enterprise.

The phrase 'any great enterprise' must surely refer to more than England's attempt at establishing a free Commonwealth. Greece and Rome had been the model for England not only in their form of government but also in the arts, and Milton's lifelong ambition of rivalling their literary achievement was subject, he believed, to the same disadvantages as had already overcome his country. *Paradise Lost* expresses similar fears lest

> an age too late, or cold
> Climate, or years damp my intended wing
> Depressed, and much they may, if all be mine,
> Not hers who brings it nightly to my ear
> (IX. 44–7).

As the last line of this quotation shows, Milton's ultimate reliance is on the Holy Spirit, or that form of it which is his Muse, to make up for such deficiencies as are the result of his personal situation or his share of the national character. But he had also done what he could to remedy these deficiencies by the study of 'foreign writers and examples of best ages'. The demand for complete originality is a comparatively modern phenomenon, and Milton's use of literary allusions was quite normal for his period. He could count on his readers' recognizing most of the references which we now rely on footnotes to explain, since most educated men had a good knowledge of the Latin authors. His knowledge of Greek and Hebrew, his exceptionally good command of Italian, and his complete lack of interest in French were more unusual. But he does not parade his knowledge of such works as his readers are unlikely to know. Good translations of both Ariosto and Tasso, for instance, were widely read in the seventeenth century. And of course everybody, even under the Restoration, was well acquainted with the Bible.

Though Milton obviously put the Bible into a different category from other books, he did not think of it simply as a religious text but also as a great work of literature. His analysis of the different literary genres in *Reason of Church Government Urged* describes the Book of the Revelation as 'a high and stately tragedy', complete with Chorus of angels, the Book of Job as a brief epic, and the poetic parts of the Old Testament as the finest lyric poetry ever written. In *Paradise Regained*, Christ rejects Satan's most persuasive temptation, the art and philosophy of Athens, declaring that the Hebrew writers surpass the Greeks in both. A similar preference made Milton begin each day, while he was composing *Paradise Lost*, by having someone read aloud to him from the Hebrew Bible.

Quotations and paraphrases of the Bible abound in Milton's work, as in many Puritan writers, and are too obvious to need pointing out. Its exotic imagery—milk and honey, the good shepherd, the river of life, jewels and spices—coloured both his verse and prose. In the language of prayer, especially, he sometimes achieves extraordinary effects, as when he calls down destruction on the enemies of true religion: 'Let them decree, and do thou cancel it; let them gather themselves, and be scattered; let them embattle themselves, and be broken; let them embattle, and be broken, for thou art with us' (*Of Reformation*, 1641). Here, in prose, Milton comes much closer to the style of Old Testament poetry (and, in this case, to Old Testament bloodthirstiness as well) than in his various attempts at translating the psalms into English rhymed verse. The most successful of these, which he did in 1653, are the least regular in form; he seems to have been experimenting, in an attempt to capture the varied and subtle effects of Hebrew poetry.

In his search for new metres, Milton was a belated Elizabethan. There had been a number of sixteenth-century attempts, Spenser's among them, at producing an English poetry based on the Greek and Latin *quantities* (the pattern of long and short syllables in a line) rather than stress. Many writers before Milton had also grown irritated at the constricting effects of rhyme, which often forced the poet to sacrifice precision of meaning to smoothness of sound. Ben Jonson wrote a 'Fit of Rhyme Against Rhyme', accusing it of

> Wresting words from their true calling,
> Propping verse for fear of falling
>   To the ground;
> Jointing syllabes, drowning letters,
> Fast'ning vowels as with fetters
>   They were bound!

But Jonson obviously enjoys showing how well he can cope with the difficulties about which he is complaining. Except in his satiric sonnets, Milton never took that kind of pleasure in exploiting the English language's shortage of rhymes. Nor, in fact, did other poets after the Metaphysicals. Though Miltonic blank verse did not catch on until the following century, the movement was generally away from the involved stanza forms to simpler couplets and quatrains where the rhymes, except when called upon for a special comic or dramatic effect, were expected only to supply an unobtrusive musical accompaniment to the poet's ideas.

It was in the Italian poets that Milton found the most interesting examples of experiment within the conventions of rhyme. F. T. Prince has shown, in his study of *The Italian Element in Milton's Verse*, that Italian verse forms were influencing him even before his trip to Italy. The unusual form of *Lycidas*, with its lines and stanzas of irregular length and its equally irregular recurrence of rhyme, is that of the Italian *canzone*. The sixteenth-century poets Bembo, Della Casa and Tasso, fascinated, like the Elizabethans, with the possibilities of imitating the classics in their own language, had found ways of giving Italian verse something of the same compression and difficulty as Latin without resorting to unfamiliar metres. They used as distorted a word order as possible, made frequent use of elision (the running of two vowel sounds together, as in 'th' heavenly'), and let the verse flow from one line to the next without pause, thus creating a tension between the natural rhythm of the poem and the speech rhythm which the reader had to use in order to bring out the meaning. Milton's Italian sonnets show that he was acquainted with these writers and he carried over many of their devices into English.

It may also have been in Italian that Milton found the precedent for writing a blank verse epic, since there had been few previous English examples of blank verse used outside the drama. Though Tasso's great work, the epic *Jerusalem Delivered*, was written in *ottava rima* (an eight-line rhyming stanza), he used blank verse for a poem on the creation of the world, and the form was also used by other Italian writers.

Critics sometimes point out that many Augustan attempts at blank verse sound just like unrhymed heroic couplets: that is, the thought falls within the individual line unit rather than overlapping from line to line. Milton took a great deal of trouble to avoid this kind of monotony in his epic verse, and succeeded so well that most readers do not even notice the occasional rhymes which he seems inadvertently to have allowed into *Paradise Lost* (the most striking example is Beelzebub's first speech—I. 143–52—where 'entire', 'ire', and 'fire' appear within seven lines). These show how powerful is the instinct to rhyme in English—stronger, in fact, than in languages where it is easier to do—but do not detract from the sense of vastness which Milton, like the Italians, wanted to achieve.

References to Milton's 'Latinate diction' usually mean one of three things: the use of English words in their original Latin meaning, the writing of English with Latin grammatical constructions ('After the Tuscan mariners transformed' instead of 'After the Tuscan mariners had been transformed', for instance), or the use of Latin word order. The first of these is true of other languages as well as of Latin: Milton uses the original French meaning of 'puny' (*puis né*, or born later—*PL* II. 367) and the Italian *all'arme* (ready for battle) lies behind his description of 'Satan alarmed' (*PL* IV. 985). It is increasingly being realized that many of Milton's supposed Latinisms are normal seventeenth-century usage. The same is true of some, though not all, of his grammatical constructions.

His prose sentences are sometimes described as Latinate simply because they are long. But the following sentence, from the famous autobiographical digression in *Reason of Church Government Urged*, is perfectly English in its word order and typical of its period in its elaborately parenthetical development. Its apparent ramblings (which become clearer if one reads it aloud) are actually designed to mirror the gradual growth of the 'inward prompting' which Milton describes.

> But much latelier in the private Academies of Italy, whither I was favoured to resort, perceiving that some trifles which I had in memory, composed at under twenty or thereabout (for the manner is that every one must give some proof of his wit and reading there) met with acceptance above what was looked for, and other things which I had shifted in scarcity of books and conveniences to patch up amongst them, were received with written Encomiums, which the Italian is not forward to bestow on men of this side the Alps, I began thus far to assent both to them and divers of my friends here at home, and not less to an inward prompting which now grew daily upon me, that by labour and intent study (which I take to be my portion in this life) joined with the strong propensity of nature, I might perhaps leave something so written to aftertimes, as they should not willingly let it die.

The sentence hesitates because Milton hesitates; it would be hard to imagine a more timid way of announcing that you have decided to write a masterpiece. When he wants to be more direct, however, he knows how to do it: 'We boast our light; but if we look not wisely on the sun itself, it smites us into darkness' (*Areopagitica*). If Milton's prose at its best can be called Latinate at all, it is only because, like that of the Latin writers, it is based on the rhythms of the speaking voice and meant to be heard.

Because English is not an inflected language like Latin, it is tied to a relatively fixed word order ('John loves Mary' becomes a different statement if one writes 'Mary loves John'). Only the personal pronouns, which have an accusative and genitive as well as a nominative case, allow inversions without the danger of ambiguity. Milton is rather fond of this type of construction and sometimes uses 'Me' at the beginning of a sentence as a kind of shorthand for 'As for me, I . . .'. But his manipulation of normal word order can combine with his loose sentence structure to produce disastrous effects. Here, for example, is the second sentence of *Areopagitica*:

> And me perhaps each of these dispositions, as the subject was whereon I entered, may have at other times variously affected; and likely might in these foremost expressions now also disclose

which of them swayed most, but that the very attempt of this address thus made, and the thought of whom it hath recourse to, hath got the power within me to a passion, far more welcome than incidental to a preface.

This is Milton's prose at its worst; the word order is so distorted as to make the meaning hard to follow and the participial phrase 'the very attempt of this address thus made' is an awkward Latinism. But in one respect the sentence suffers from not being Latinate enough; like much other seventeenth-century prose, it lacks a sense of form.

He is able to be much freer with the word order in his verse, where this sense of form is supplied by the rhythm of the lines. Inversions are especially common in the more personal passages of *Paradise Lost*:

> Yet not the more
> Cease I to wander where the Muses haunt
> Clear spring, or shady grove, or sunny hill,
> Smit with the love of sacred song; but chief
> Thee Sion and the flowery brooks beneath
> That wash thy hallowed feet, and warbling flow,
> Nightly I visit
>   (III. 26–32).

If one contrasts this with the style of Satan ('I therefore, I alone first undertook/ To wing the desolate abyss') it is apparent that Milton has very carefully arranged to stress 'Thee' and bury the 'I' as applied to himself in a mass of qualifying phrases, while emphasizing the egotism in Satan's use of the same word. Satan's 'I's fall on stressed syllables; Milton's do not. Where possible, he replaces 'I' by the accusative:

> Me of these
> Nor skilled nor studious, higher argument
> Remains
>   (IX. 41–3).

This is because his aim throughout is to represent himself not as an author but as a recipient of divine inspiration.

Milton was not just being perverse in trying to avoid a too-easy style; he wanted to be read carefully, as one has to read the Latin authors. Anyone who tries to read his blank verse aloud—and this is certainly the best way to read it—is likely to run into difficulties at first. Many of these result from its extreme condensation. The language is so loaded with significance that it is hard to see where to put the stress; every word seems to demand it. Sentences don't stop where one expects them to, but run on, sometimes leaving a stray clause apparently attached to two places at once. Or—this is a favourite trick of Milton's—having come to the end of a line and taken a deep breath, one finds that the beginning of the next line cancels out what has gone before: 'thus they relate, Erring' (*PL* I. 746–7). These are deliberate surprises, meant to keep the reader on his guard. And difficult syntax usually goes with the description of difficult action or the depiction of complex emotions in a speaker. None of this matters very much after a while: the main thing, as in Satan's flight through Chaos, is to keep going.

Milton and English poetry

Milton's constant assimilation of whatever he considered permanent and beautiful in classical and foreign literature links him with Spenser and other poets of the late Elizabethan age rather than with the literary fashions of his own time. To appreciate just how far removed he was from his contemporaries, one need only look at Thomas Carew's verses on the death of John Donne, published in 1633. Donne, he says, rescued English poetry from the 'servile imitation' of the classics, pedantic language and hackneyed subject matter; his works would have impressed even 'good Old Orpheus' and 'all the ancient Brood Our superstitious fools admire'. Alas, he goes on, now that Donne is dead a new generation of poets will undo all his work:

> They will repeal the goodly exiled train
> Of gods and goddesses, which in thy just reign
> Were banished nobler Poems, now, with these
> The silenced tales o' the Metamorphoses
> Shall stuff their lines, and swell the windy Page.

This is, in fact, exactly what happened. The movement towards a more classical poetry was on foot before the Restoration, due in part to the influence of French literature and literary theory. But it was not Milton's kind of classicism. The poets of the Restoration and early eighteenth century retained something of the colloquial ease and urbanity of the metaphysicals even as they refined on what they, sometimes mistakenly, believed to be rough versification and difficult scansion. Though they imitated Milton's manner in their serious poems, his influence was most pronounced, and most successfully absorbed, in the mock-heroic tradition. In fact, Carew's flippant reference to 'good Old Orpheus', so different from Milton's own deeply personal involvement with that myth (see p. 151), really anticipates the Restoration manner.

Milton's ability to use the classical myths seriously, and in the context of Christian poetry, is one which he shares with other Renaissance poets, notably Spenser, whose *Faerie Queene* places the Greek Tantalus and the biblical Pontius Pilate side by side in a classical hell. He is indebted to 'our sage and serious Spenser', whom *Areopagitica* also calls 'a better teacher than Scotus or Aquinas', not only for much of the subject matter of *Comus* (the enchanter, the story of Sabrina, and the Garden of Adonis) but also for the moral atmosphere of many descriptive passages in *Paradise Lost.* The contrast between Pandemonium (artificial lighting, elaborate manmade decoration, a great crowd gathered indoors) and the Garden of Eden (fresh air, emphasis on the exuberance and wildness of nature as opposed to 'nice art'—IV. 241) is, as in Spenser's similar treatment of the House of Busirane and the Garden of Adonis, more than just an aesthetic one. It is in the Spenserian tradition of sensuous beauty, musical verse, and the use of allegory to harmonize pagan and Christian themes, that Milton most clearly belongs.

Though much of Donne's verse dates from the same period as *The Faerie Queene*, the fact that it was not published until 1633 but only circulated in manuscript caused his influence to be felt a generation later than Spenser's. It became fashionable to use the tricks of Donne's style (the underlying seriousness usually eluded his imitators) for a poetry of wild hyperboles, cynicism, and ingenious comparisons or 'conceits'. This manner also affected the so-called 'Tribe of Ben', young admirers of Ben Jonson who called themselves his 'sons' and tried to achieve his urbane conversational style in poems of friendship, gallantry and the good life. Jonson's favourite classical authors were the social critics, especially Horace, rather than the more romantic writers, Ovid and Virgil in particular, who interested Milton. The tone of much early seventeenth-century poetry is satirical, about love as well as about society, and the cynical sensuality of Donne's lighter love poems combined with Jonson's scholarly evocation of a man's world to produce, in the 'Cavalier' poets who were Milton's contemporaries, a poetry whose attitude to women was cavalier in more ways than one.

Disturbed by the amount of talent that was going into the writing of libertine verses, some writers wondered whether religious poetry could not be given the same beauty and intensity. Both Donne and Herbert were aware of the relationship between love of woman and love of God. In one of his Holy Sonnets Donne uses to God an argument which, he admits, he has already tried on 'all my profane mistresses'. Herbert, in a poem addressed to God, asks,

> Why are not sonnets made of thee, and lays
> Upon thy altar burnt? Cannot thy love
> Heighten a spirit to sound out thy praise
> As well as any she?

In *The Temple* (1633), he tried to fulfil this need. The volume is designed like a church, with poems arising from the contemplation of various parts of the building, commemorating the festivals in the church calendar, and recording the ups and downs of the author's spiritual life.

Both the love poetry and the religious poetry of Donne and the other metaphysicals is based on conflict, usually arising out of a sense of sin: the poet loves but despises his mistress, or despises himself for loving, or despises the world for not understanding his love; he loves but yet fears God, he has faith and yet is terrified that his sins may be too great for forgiveness. Even the comparatively serene Herbert goes through periods of bleak depression and sometimes rebels against the demands of a totally dedicated religious life. Man's mortality preoccupies these writers. Like the Jacobean dramatists, they like to talk of graves, of worms, of epitaphs. Their insistence on the ugly physical reality of death differentiates them from the Greek and Latin poets, whose *carpe diem* theme ('seize the day' — that is, enjoy life while you can) depends on a strong awareness of death but holds it at a distance.

Not only Milton's sense of dignity but his belief in mankind as a whole keeps him from writing of human beings as worms, miserable sinners, creatures born to die and so on. We have seen that his opposition to Anglican church government was based on the conviction that men were capable of acting virtuously through the grace of God in them, and did not have to be cajoled or terrorized into it by a member of the church hierarchy. Both Donne and Herbert, one should remember, were members of that hierarchy and well thought of by Laud. Donne, moreover, had been brought up as a Roman Catholic and once admitted that his morbid tendencies might have been fostered in him by a childhood in which the possibility of martyrdom for the sake of religion was frequently discussed. Herbert, who had taken orders on Laud's persuasion, restored and beautified two churches and, during the short period of his ministry, tried to make himself not only the spiritual guide of his parish but also its doctor and lawyer—the man, in fact, that people would turn to on any occasion. The effect of this saintly behaviour could only be to strengthen the church's hold on the secular life of the community, which, of course, is precisely what Laud wanted to see happen.

Of the other well-known metaphysical religious poets, Henry King (the brother of 'Lycidas') was an Anglican bishop, Henry Vaughan a devout Anglican and Royalist, and Richard Crashaw (though the son of a Puritan divine) a Royalist and convert to Roman Catholicism. It is not surprising that Milton's poetry is so very different in tone. Only his friend Marvell can be said to have shared his independent religious views, but Marvell had been Royalist and even, briefly, a Catholic before he gave his allegiance to the Commonwealth. Both he and Milton wrote poems to Cromwell, but the elaborate ambiguities of Marvell's *Horatian Ode* are the product of a much more complex attitude than that of Milton's sonnet.

The Heavenly Muse who inspired Milton's poetry, then, is not related to the spirit of his age. If anything, she is Elizabethan. The French poet Du Bartas, whose works were translated by Joshuah Sylvester between 1592 and 1605, described how she appeared to him after he had been engaged in a long search for fame through worldly writings:

> I am Urania (then aloud said she)
> Who humankind above the poles transport,
> Teaching their hands to touch, and eyes to see
> All the intercourse of the Celestial Court.

Inspired by her, he turned to the writing of poetry on religious subjects, of which the most famous was his *Divine Works and Days*, an account of the creation of the world and fall of man. Other writers of religious poetry also dedicated their works to Urania. Their subject matter was taken from the Scriptures and, although they generally embroidered it with commentary and personal digressions, the followers of the Heavenly Muse differed from the metaphysical poets in that they were not writing primarily about their own spiritual conflicts.

Such inner conflicts as appear in Milton's work differ from those of the metaphysicals in that they arise out of the clash of a righteous man with an unrighteous world rather than with his own weaknesses and vices. The consistency of his personal and poetic development meant that, unlike Donne, he never felt the desire to suppress any of his earlier works. Except for the sonnets too directly related to events under the Commonwealth, which could not very well be published after the Restoration, he saw to it that all his poetic works, however immature or unsuccessful, were in print before his death. The care with which the poems are arranged in the 1645 and 1673 editions shows that Milton thought of his works as a continuous whole. Poems of love give way to poems of friendship as the poet gets older, but this transition is not accompanied by remorse or self-loathing.

Thus Milton does not present sensual love as if it were a real temptation to him. In *Lycidas*, for example, he is not torn between his duty to poetry and religion on the one hand and his desire to 'sport with Amaryllis in the shade' on the other; he simply wonders why he has reaped no reward for his dedication. His love poems— which, except for *Sonnet I*, are all either in Latin or Italian — treat the idea of woman with respect but are quite free of any sense of inferiority to her; indeed, he sometimes seems to be saying that Cupid and the lady between them ought to congratulate themselves on having caught such a strong-minded young man. The Latin *Elegy VII* was the only one which he felt obliged to retract later on, presumably because here he allows himself to speculate whether the unknown girl with whom he has fallen in love at first sight might prove more compliant on further acquaintance. 'These lines are the trifling memorials of my youth,' he explained in Latin verses added to the 1645 edition, and he went on to say that Venus and Cupid were now terrified of him, since he had become a follower of Plato. But the facetious tone of these lines, and the fact that he did, after all, print *Elegy VII*, shows that he cannot have regarded it as seriously to be condemned. He was simply indicating that he had moved one stage on in his development.

According to the doctrine of Platonic love, the lover begins by loving one person and then discovers that all earthly goodness and beauty is only a reflection of an ideal that cannot be found on the earth. Christian writers, especially Dante and Petrarch, later developed this idea into a kind of love poetry (usually known as Petrarchan) in which the woman became for her lover a symbol of divine beauty and goodness. It was in this spirit that Milton wrote his Italian sonnets; in *Sonnet II*, for instance, he tells the lady that only a worthless person could fail to fall in love with her. In other words, it is her goodness that calls forth his own love of goodness.

But it need not be, as for Petrarch and his successors it was, an unattainable ideal, resulting in a frustrated and unhappy love. It was this aspect of Petrarchanism that the anti-platonic poets of the seventeenth century reacted against by insisting on the importance of the senses and proclaiming their contempt for any woman who refused to let herself be seduced. Milton, like Spenser, believed that marriage was the only satisfactory way of reconciling man's sensual and spiritual needs; the love of husband and wife for each other would help them both to love God better. In a sonnet written on Easter Day, Spenser reminds his wife of God's love for man and concludes,

> So let us love, dear love, like as we ought:
> Love is the lesson which the Lord us taught.

This idealization of marriage, as opposed to the unfulfilled love of the Petrarchan sonneteer, is related to Puritanism in so far as it makes the family the centre of religious life. That it caught Milton's imagination is evident. Even his early drafts for a drama on the fall of man include Heavenly Love among the cast of characters and call for a chorus of angels to sing Adam and Eve's marriage song. The divorce pamphlets give plenty of evidence that Milton soon came to know the difficulty of achieving the perfect harmony which constituted his idea of marriage, but *Sonnet XIX* ('Methought I saw my late espoused saint') suggests that the ideal relationship of Adam and Eve in *Paradise Lost* did not have to be drawn entirely from his imagination.

In a somewhat similar way, Milton's use of pastoral begins with a delight in the beauty of nature, described in a stylized, traditional way, and ends by seeing it as a symbol of the perfect harmony of heaven. The opening line of *Paradise Regained* places *Paradise Lost* in the category of pastoral, calling it a poem about 'the happy garden'. This seems an extraordinary description at first, but it is true that a large part of the epic is about the lives of Adam and Eve in a situation which corresponds to the Golden Age of classical pastoral. The outdoor meal of Adam, Eve and Raphael in Book V is clearly in the same tradition as the country scene in *L'Allegro*,

Where Corydon and Thyrsis met,
Are at their savoury dinner set
Of herbs, and other country messes,
Which the neat-handed Phillis dresses;
And then in haste her bower she leaves,
With Thestylis to bind the sheaves
                    (83–8).

The parallel holds even in the fact that in both cases the woman departs early, leaving the men to their conversation.

'Long choosing, and beginning late' on his great epic, Milton was probably attracted to the pastoral genre because it was traditionally associated with the early stages of a poet's development. Spenser, for instance, had inaugurated his poetic career with the publication of *The Shepherd's Calendar* (1579), more than ten years before he brought out the first part of *The Faerie Queene*. According to the friend who wrote the dedicatory epistle, Spenser was deliberately 'following the example of the best and most ancient poets, which devised this kind of writing, being both so base for the matter and homely for the manner, at the first to try their abilities'. He was thinking mainly of Virgil, who wrote his *Eclogues* and *Georgics* before going on to the *Aeneid*. Milton, as we have seen, brought out his 1645 *Poems* in a format suggesting that they were pastorals, and this seems as good a description as any for poems in which nymphs and singing shepherds so often appear.

Why pastoral was so popular for so long (it is thought to have originated with the Greek poet Theocritus in the third century B.C.) is hard to say. One reason, however, must be its versatility. The shepherds who inhabit its idealized Sicilian or Arcadian landscapes do not confine themselves to holding song contests, watching their sheep, or bewailing their unsuccessful loves. Under cover of their apparent simplicity they are also able to comment on the events of their own times. Thus, Virgil's *Eclogues* allude to both Julius and Augustus Caesar, and Spenser used his *Shepherd's Calendar* to praise Queen Elizabeth, satirize the Catholic Church, and bemoan the poverty of poets. Sidney's *Arcadia* and Shakespeare's *As You Like It* are among the many works in which aristocratic characters are brought into a pastoral setting which is both compared and contrasted with the court.

Perhaps the most effective use of pastoral was as a vehicle for lamenting the death of a friend. The country setting lent itself to simple and beautiful comparisons between nature's cycle of death and rebirth and the brevity of man's life. From this followed also the so-called 'pathetic fallacy', the pretence that all nature was mourning along with the poet. In Christian tradition, of course, the theme of human mortality is qualified by belief in the resurrection, but the classical poets had also found a way of introducing the idea of consolation and recompense. After one of Virgil's shepherds has mourned the death of young Daphnis, another sings of his ascending into the heavens and becoming a god. Similarly, the first part of Spenser's November Eclogue in *The Shepherd's Calendar* mourns the death of 'Dido', with the refrain 'O carefull verse!' but then the poet reminds himself that she is not really dead after all. She is walking in the Elysian fields:

> Fair fields and pleasant lays there been,
> The fields ay fresh, the grass ay green . . .
> There lives she with the blessed gods in bliss,
> There drinks she nectar with ambrosia mixed,
> And joys enjoys that mortal men do miss.

And the refrain, accordingly, changes to 'Oh joyfull verse!'

There is thus scarcely any feature of *Lycidas* that cannot be paralleled in some other pastoral elegy. Even the idea of the song contest may be present, since the poem was written as part of a collection and Milton may have thought of himself as competing with the writers of the other elegies. Most of these were more or less metaphysical in manner. His one reference to the kind of poetry which they represented seems to be the phrase 'our late fantastics' in the verse speech which he made at a Cambridge vacation gathering. Yet some of his own poems are sufficiently 'fantastic' to have been included in well-known anthologies of metaphysical poetry by H. J. C. Grierson, Helen Gardner and others. And some of them are Horatian, though not in the sense that the Cavalier poets gave to the word. Examples of both these styles are discussed in Part II. Nevertheless, the development of Milton's poetry is further and further away from that of his own time. The ending of *Lycidas* is symbolic in several ways. Not only does it draw our attention away from the song to the singer, and tell us that he is about to go somewhere else, it also makes us aware of his isolation. The man who has conjured up Neptune, Camus, and St Peter turns out to have been singing only to the 'oak and rills'. Already, it would seem, Milton had decided that his poetic audience, if it was to be fit, would also have to be few.

Masque and drama

Milton's attitude to the drama of his day is that of a poet rather than a man with any strong sense of theatre. We know from *L'Allegro* that, unlike the conventional Puritan, he could approve of going to the playhouse

> If Jonson's learned sock be on,
> Or sweetest Shakespeare fancy's child,
> Warble his native wood-notes wild
>
> (132–4).

But in the context of *L'Allegro* this means that he is thinking only of the comedies of these playwrights. When, in *Il Penseroso*, he is in the mood for 'gorgeous Tragedy', it is to the Greeks and Romans that he turns, with a brief mention of

> what (though rare) of later age,
> Ennobled hath the buskined stage
> (101–2).

And even these later plays may not be Shakespeare's, as we would expect, but rather the sixteenth-century Italian drama which he praises, in the preface to *Samson Agonistes*, for using a chorus in the manner of the Greeks. Since he was prepared to write a new *Macbeth*, he can hardly have felt that the definitive work on that subject had already appeared.

Milton's contrast of Jonson's learning with the inspired naïvety of Shakespeare is the conventional one of the seventeenth century, derived probably from Jonson's elegy in the First Folio which mentions his colleague's 'small Latin and less Greek'. The phrase 'native wood-notes wild' makes Shakespeare sound like a pastoral singer, and this may have been how Milton thought of him. Certainly, it is his lighter, more lyrical side that is most obviously reflected in Milton's early work. There are recognizable echoes of *A Midsummer Night's Dream* and *The Tempest* in *Comus*, and the flower passage of *Lycidas*, particularly in Milton's first draft, owes a great deal to Perdita's lovely catalogue of flowers in Act IV of *The Winter's Tale*. Milton knew most of Shakespeare's plays, of course, and his verbal reminiscences of the histories and tragedies can also be found here and there, but it is not until his later works that he shows any sign of having absorbed their dramatic quality. As late as 1649—though admittedly in the blatantly partisan context of *Eikonoklastes*—he could mention Charles I's reading of Shakespeare in his imprisonment in order to imply that the King had a trivial mind.

Shakespeare died when Milton was only a child, but Jonson lived until 1637 and held court in the Mermaid Tavern, just down the street from Milton's home. Whether or not Milton ever saw the old poet, he would certainly have heard a lot about him, as Jonson was usually engaged in some well-publicized literary quarrel—in 1631 he and Milton's friend Alexander Gill exchanged insults in verse. To praise Jonson for his classical learning was the thing to do in the seventeenth century, and Milton no doubt approved of his satiric comedies and his two tragedies in the Roman manner which, like most such attempts in this period, had been unsuccessful on the stage. But it was to the lyrical Jonson of the masques, not the satirical Jonson of the plays, that he was most drawn.

Both Shakespeare and Jonson were being acted up to the closing of the theatres in 1642, so if Milton started going to the theatre while in his teens he could have seen most of the great Elizabethan

88

and Jacobean plays. Fletcher's *Faithful Shepherdess* (1608) may well
have influenced *Comus;* it is a pastoral drama in rhymed verse,
partly inspired by Italian examples, and it treats chastity as a virtue
which gives its possessor magic powers. *The Old Wives Tale* (1592)
is like *Comus* in its basic story—two brothers looking for their sister
who has been captured by an enchanter—but it is more likely that
Milton was drawing on a common source in folklore than that he
actually knew this old play. One would like to know whether he
had read Marlowe's *Dr Faustus* (*c.* 1592), the earliest English play
to explore damnation. It used to be assumed that Satan's 'Which
way I fly is hell, myself am hell' (*PL* IV. 75) was inspired by the
words of Marlowe's Mephistopheles:

> Hell hath no limits, nor is circumscribed
> In one self place; but where we are is hell.

But this concept of hell might equally well have come from (among
many possible sources) Thomas Browne's *Religio Medici*—'every
Devil is an Hell unto himself'—or Fairfax's translation of Tasso's
Jerusalem Delivered:

> Swift from myself I run, myself I fear,
> Yet still my hell within myself I bear.

The qualities which make Satan 'the last great tragic figure in our
literature' may, as Helen Gardner suggests in *A Reading of Paradise
Lost*, be a result of his kinship with Faustus, Macbeth, and other
evil yet noble heroes of this great age of drama. But it was not until
late in his life that Milton came to the intimate understanding of
human suffering which made it possible for him to create such a
character.

The early 1630s were probably the period of his keenest theatre-
going, since it was at this time that he knew the composer Henry
Lawes and was involved in the writing of *Arcades* and *Comus*. The
Caroline dramatists did not have much to offer him in their rather
bloodless verse and their mechanical portrayal of love and honour
in conflict. The sensationalism and occasional sadism of this type of
drama must have been particularly distasteful to a writer who, as
has often been noticed, consistently avoids dwelling on the subject
of physical suffering even in contexts (Hell, for instance) where it
seems an inevitable part of his subject. Yet scholars have found an
echo in *Paradise Regained* of the phrase 'grey dissimulation' from
Ford's *The Broken Heart* (*c.* 1633). If Milton really did remember this
expression, more than thirty years later, it may have been because
Ford's play, which has a classical setting, caught his youthful
imagination with its idealized characters and its use of music and
the dance for symbolic effect. In the most famous scene of the play,
the princess Calantha is told successively of the deaths of her father,
friend, and lover, but insists (though she dies later of a broken
heart) on continuing the dance which is in progress at the time and
which stands for harmony in her court.

The original music for Comus, *by Henry Lawes*

Goddess of the Silver Lake Listen Listen and save.

Back Shepherds Back enough Your Play till the next Sunshine

Holiday Here be without Duck or nod other trippings to be trod

of lighter Toes & such Court Guise as Mercury did first devise with ye mincing

Dryades O're the Lawns & o're the Seas   Exeunt   Noble Lord & Lady

bright I have brought You new delight Here behold So goodly grown

Three fair Branches of Your own Heav'n hath timely try'd their Youth their

Faith their Patience & their Truth and sent them here thro' hard Assays

This concept of the dance as a symbol of the order and harmony of a hierarchical universe is the basis of the masque, and explains why so expensive and aristocratic an art form was nevertheless attractive to a sober young man like Milton. In its simplest form, masquing originated in the surprise visit, to a banquet or revel, of dancers in disguise. In the early seventeenth century it took much more elaborate forms: the dancers gave their performance on a stage with scenery, and the entertainment was built round a simple story. Music and song became more important; in fact, the total effect was a union of all the arts, much like Italian opera. But the masque differed from both opera and drama in two important respects: it was built round the dance rather than the spoken word, and the chief performers were not professionals but noble lords and ladies showing their mastery of what was supposed to be a specifically aristocratic accomplishment. Professional performers were also called in to take part in the court masques but their roles were sharply differentiated from those of the amateurs; they played buffoons or grotesques and were eventually driven off by the noble dancers. It was a very class-conscious art form.

It was Ben Jonson who first found a way of giving an artistic unity to this series of dances by turning the performance into an allegory of the triumph of virtue over vice. The professional dancers, or anti-masquers, appeared at the beginning of the performance, establishing themselves as comic figures but also symbols of vice. Then the masquers proper—that is, the noble performers, playing virtues of which they were supposed to be the incarnation in real life—would reveal themselves. The very sight of them was enough to banish the forces of evil without a struggle. Sometimes it was the sight of the audience, especially if the king or queen was present, that effected the miraculous victory of good.

The masque always concluded, in any case, with the masquers not only recognizing their audience but becoming part of it as the performance dissolved into a series of dances, intricate and difficult (we are told that they often took up to a month to rehearse), which symbolized the re-established harmony of society and the 'mystic dance' of the stars. The angels themselves, Raphael declares in *Paradise Lost*, imitate both the music and the motion of the spheres in their

> mazes intricate,
> Eccentric, intervolved, yet regular
> Then most, when most irregular they seem,
> And in their motions harmony divine
> So smooths her charming tones, that God's own ear
> Listens delighted
>
> (*PL* V. 622–7).

Comus and his crew also try to 'imitate the starry quire' (112), but they are only the antimasquers of Milton's performance. The true mystic dance occurs at the end, when Lord Brackley, Mr Thomas

Lady Alice Egerton, the heroine of Comus

Egerton, and Lady Alice Egerton are led before their parents by the Attendant Spirit,

> To triumph in victorious dance
> O'er sensual folly, and intemperance
> (*PL* V. 973–4).

The most luxurious and spectacular masques were the ones that Jonson and Inigo Jones devised for performance at court. In their grand transformation scenes, rocks opened to become palaces, gods descended from above on clouds, and revolving machinery enabled almost instantaneous changes of set. The magic effect was enhanced by the dim candlelight which could give way to a sudden blaze as a troop of torchbearers entered (the Egerton brothers had made their stage debuts in this role). Candles behind bowls of coloured water gave a dancing light and reflected off the spangled costumes of the masquers. J. G. Demaray's *Milton and the Masque Tradition* suggests that the poet's acquaintance with the techniques of masque production can be seen in such details as the 'spangled host' of angels in the *Nativity Ode* and the description of Mercy descending from above, as if on one of Jones's machines,

> Throned in celestial sheen,
> With radiant feet the tissued clouds down steering
> (145–6).

Most of these elaborate effects were probably beyond the means of the family of the Earl of Bridgewater. *Arcades*, or at least the part of it to which Milton contributed, certainly seems a simple entertainment. Members of the Countess of Derby's family, in elegant shepherds' (Arcadians') costume, entered her presence, pretended to take her for a goddess or 'rural queen', and performed songs and dances in her honour. Henry Lawes, playing a 'Genius of the wood', led them toward the old lady 'O'er the smooth enamelled green', which probably means the green cloth with which the floor of the masquing hall was usually covered.

Puritan attacks on the theatre often made much of the fact that the Greek word for actor had the same root as 'hypocrite'; all acting, they maintained, was a form of dissembling. If challenged on this point, Milton could have replied that in his two courtly entertainments no dissembling was involved on the part of the noble performers: they played themselves. The setting in each case is real, not imaginary: a wood on the estate at Harefield (which had a real lane of elm trees like the one mentioned by the Genius of the Wood), or a forest near Ludlow Castle. The shepherds in *Arcades* are at once recognized as being of noble birth, and the children in *Comus* are portrayed in their real-life relationship to Henry Lawes. At the beginning of the masque Lawes tells the audience that the Egerton children are travelling home through the forest in order to be with their family on an evening of festivity. The festivity is, of course, the masque itself, in which the audience sees them on their journey. At the end of the performance, all that is required to move them from the dark wood to their father's palace is that they become conscious of the audience which has been there all along.

This personal and topical element in the masque is the hardest thing for us to recapture today. Masques were never given more than once, for one particular occasion. The published accounts of the performance give their stage directions in the past tense; they are intended for a reader who wants to re-create the experience in his own mind, not for a producer to imitate on some other occasion. Because much of the visual effect of the production depended on surprise, masque costumes and scenery were unusable, at court anyway, after one appearance. They could, however, be hired out to amateurs, and it is possible that the subject of *Comus* may have been partly dictated to Milton by the kinds of costumes available. To judge from his stage directions, he was rather vague about production details: the Attendant Spirit 'descends or enters' at the beginning, for instance; obviously, Milton did not know whether the budget would run to a machine for lowering Lawes in a cloud. The fact that, even in the published version, he gives only a bare minimum of directions, instead of the usual loving description of costumes and sets that Jonson and other masque writers went in for, may mean that he was unable to see the performance himself. Or it may be his way of showing, as Jonson had shown more publicly in his quarrels with Inigo Jones, that he disliked the attention often paid to the visual part of the masque at the expense of its literary content.

Comus is no less hierarchical than other masques. The published text lists the names of the three children as 'the chief persons which presented', and we only know from Lawes's letter dedicating the masque to the elder brother that it was he who played the Attendant Spirit. The actor playing the difficult part of Comus is not thought worth naming; he was only an antimasquer, not a member of the family. (It has been suggested that Milton may have taken the part himself, but the idea is too good to be true. Surely, if he had, some Royalist pamphleteer would have got hold of the fact and used it against him later on, when Milton had begun to make theatrical expressions into terms of abuse, in the more orthodox Puritan manner.) The antimasquers are twice put to flight in this play: once, dramatically, when the two brothers burst in on Comus and his rout, and once, more graciously, when the rustics who dance in the final scene are dismissed by the Attendant Spirit at the entrance of the Egerton children:

> Back, shepherds, back, enough your play,
> Till next sunshine holiday,
> Here be without duck or nod
> Other trippings to be trod
> Of lighter toes (957–61).

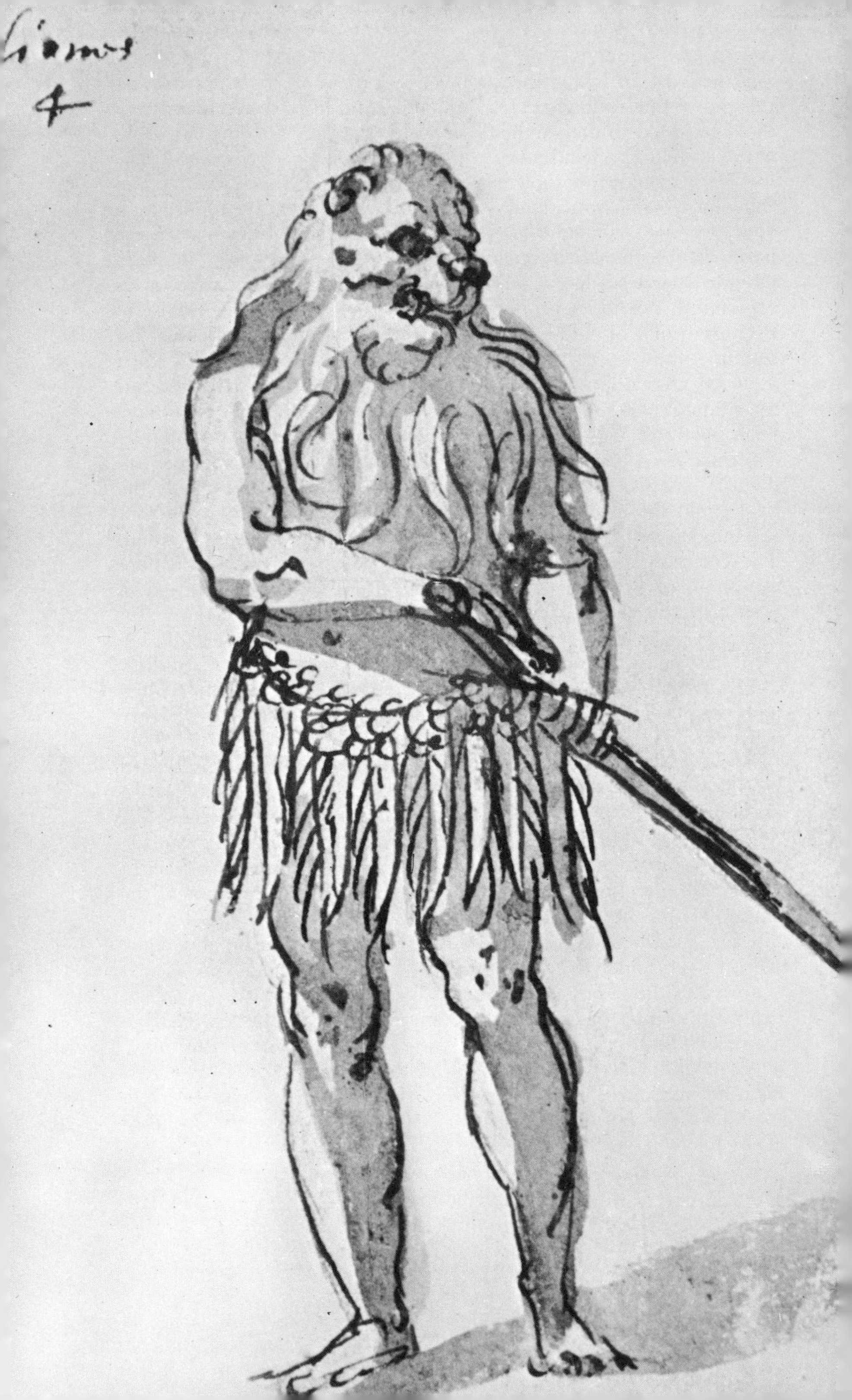
4

Milton did not need to make any concessions to the fact that his three chief performers were so young. Child actors were a familiar sight both in the professional theatre, where they performed in adult repertory, and at court; Charles I made his first appearance in a masque when he was only nine, the same age as the Younger Brother. The parts which Milton wrote for the two boys must have been more enjoyable for them to play than the personifications of virtue who, in the more conventional masque, had nothing to do except march in procession or be revealed on a dais. Their philosophical conversation on the subject of chastity may have impressed them and their parents more as a feat of memory than anything else, but they must have liked having a chance to draw their swords and do a bit of swaggering. Milton's original dialogue for them was considerably racier than in the version which he published with his poems in 1645. For instance, the Elder Brother did not merely threaten to drag Comus

> by the curls, to a foul death,
> Cursed as his life
>
> (607–8).

What he actually said in performance, no doubt with appropriate gestures, was that he wanted to

> drag him by the curls, and cleave his scalp
> Down to the hips.

When Milton, in *Paradise Lost*, refers contemptuously to the 'wanton mask' which may be a setting for illicit love (IV. 768), he is presumably thinking of large gatherings at court rather than the family party for which he had once supplied a script. Even so, the tone of this remark indicates the change in Milton's attitude to the theatre since the 1630s. His blindness, of course, would have cut him off from playgoing, even if there had been any plays to go to, in the 1650s, and it must have made him lose interest in the possibility of having his work performed. What he heard later about the Restoration theatre would not have encouraged him. Its replacement of the prewar boy actors by actresses shocked many older people who felt that women ought not to appear on the stage. Besides, it would have been one thing to put on a state-sponsored drama for the edification of a godly society, as he had suggested doing in the early 1640s, but quite another to try a revival of classical tragedy in the commercial theatre. One really cannot imagine a man like Milton submitting himself to the judgment of an ordinary first-night audience.

So, whereas the first step towards an understanding of *Comus* is to imagine the conditions of its performance—the family and friends of the Earl of Bridgewater in the candlelit hall of Ludlow Castle, admiring the improvised stage and hoping that the children would manage to remember their lines—for *Samson Agonistes* such details

Costume by Inigo Jones for Townshend's Tempe Restored, 1634   97

are irrelevant. The work, Milton says in his preface, was never meant for the stage. The reader has to become as blind as Samson, seeing the characters only through the Chorus's description of them. As with the chained Prometheus of Aeschylus's play or the blind hero of Sophocles's *Oedipus at Colonus*, the drama is focused entirely on one figure to whom all the other characters have to come. It might also be compared with the *Book of Job*, whose hero, similarly fixed in one place, is visited by a series of wouldbe comforters hoping to learn something about the ways of God to men. Neither Job's nor Samson's story formed part of the medieval drama cycles based on the Bible. Perhaps they were thought too disturbing to be performed in front of a popular audience. Besides, a popular treatment of the Samson story, whether medieval or Elizabethan, would have required a lot of spectacular stage effects. Samson is one of the most physically active characters in the Bible; part of the fascination of Milton's play, like that of some Baroque architecture and sculpture, is the sense it gives of strength and motion implicit in the stillness of the central figure.

Milton observes the unities of time, place and action in *Samson* not only to conform to the ideal of classical tragedy but also to emphasize the extent to which the hero's consciousness is the unifying force in the play. The Chorus, Manoah, Dalila, and Harapha are more like voices in his mind than characters; only at the end, after Samson has gone out, does the Chorus become spokesman for the audience. The difficulty of this audience identification with the hero is that it is most intense in his darkest moments and least so at the crucial point in the play where he becomes aware of God's spirit working through him. This kind of experience—he only describes it as some 'rousing motions' in himself—is by its nature incommunicable, and it seems from the Messenger's speech that Samson did not understand its full meaning until just before he pulled the pillars down. Thus the Chorus at the end, like the audience, are left on the outside of a religious experience that can only be meaningful to the person who has it. As with the Book of Job, the cosmic questions that have been raised receive, not a rational answer, but an affirmation of the greatness and mysteriousness of God.

Greek tragedies frequently end on such a note; the attempts of later commentators to find any justice in the fates of heroes like Oedipus overlook the fact that Greek religious drama was intended to make men fear, not love, their gods. Aristotle described the effect of tragedy as a *catharsis*, or purging, of pity and fear. There has been much debate as to whether he meant by this that the audience, at the end of a performance, should feel pity and fear more fully or not at all. Milton thought the latter, to judge from his preface to *Samson*: the art of tragedy, he says, is to arouse pity, fear, and other such emotions in the audience, and then 'to temper and reduce them to just measure with a kind of delight, stirred up by reading or seeing those passions well imitated'.

Although Milton also described tragedy as 'the gravest, moralest, and most profitable of all other poems', it would seem from his account that its moral effect has less to do with its content than with its effect on the emotions of the audience. Certainly, in Greek tragedy the behaviour of both gods and heroes is often far from admirable in terms of any conceivable moral code. Our pity is aroused for the fate of the individual sufferer, our fear by the recognition of a larger power which has dictated the course of events and which, however cruel it may be, nevertheless gives a meaning to man's life.

In *Samson*, the situation is complicated by the fact that the Christian God is supposed to be good and beneficent. It has some-times been said that a Christian tragedy is impossible, because the sufferings of a good character can be only temporary and we know that he will have eternal happiness as his reward. Perhaps this is why Milton set his Christian tragedy in Old Testament times, thus depriving Samson of the consolation which might come from his awareness of a loving and compassionate Redeemer. Nothing is said of an afterlife, only of earthly fame as a reward for Samson. The audience is not reminded that Samson's sacrifice was a prototype of Christ's; the analogy was traditional, but Milton does not make it. The very irrationality of the biblical Jehovah makes him like the terrible gods of Greek tragedy who can only be worshipped and obeyed in fear.

The Chorus's final speech in the play adds the Christian idea of 'peace and consolation' to the Aristotelean 'calm of mind all passion spent'. But *Samson* is not really a consoling play. It consists almost entirely of conflicts between characters who cannot possibly under-stand each other (hence there is more declamation than real dialogue). Even the hero's death is wrapped in complexity, since Milton wants it to be self-sacrifice but not suicide. It is the same problem that Eliot faced in *Murder in the Cathedral*, and Milton finds the same solution, describing Samson as

> self-killed
> Not willingly, but tangled in the fold
> Of dire necessity
>
> (1664–6).

He leaves it in doubt at last whether the Israelites will be able to rouse themselves to take advantage of the sacrifice. *Samson* is really a Christian play only in so far as the audience, by an act of faith, can accept that the hero's experience of God's grace is so over-whelming as to make it unnecessary to question God's justice. Otherwise, it is as disturbing and inconclusive as the tragedies of Euripides.

We might have been equally disturbed if Milton had carried out his original design of writing a tragedy instead of an epic about the fall of man. This is not because the ending would have been any more 'tragic'. It would, in fact, have been much like the end of the epic as it stands, except that the evils of the world would have been presented in an allegorical masque rather than described by Michael; all four of Milton's brief drafts (two of which are only cast lists) show that it would have concluded with Faith, Hope and Charity comforting Adam and the angelic chorus briefly summing up. But Milton's determination not to bring Adam and Eve onto the stage until after the Fall could only have meant that the main crisis of the play, their decision to eat the forbidden fruit, would have to be reported, not shown. Thus, as with Samson, the audience would be shut off from the hero's sin by the requirements of the unity of time and place, and from his regeneration by the sheer difficulty of dramatizing the operations of divine grace in any readily understandable form.

The fact that Adam and Eve had to be kept waiting in the wings until Act IV also made the choice of a central character difficult. In Milton's final draft it is apparent that Lucifer, a fairly minor part of the play as first envisaged, was becoming at least as important as Adam and Eve. Satan's speeches in *Paradise Lost* are the most theatrical parts of the poem, and many of them seem to have started as dramatic fragments (particularly his first·soliloquy in Book IV, his scene with Gabriel, his soliloquy before entering the serpent in Book IX, and perhaps his triumphant speech to the other fallen angels in Book X). Not only would Lucifer have been a powerful figure in the drama, he would also have been kept in the forefront of the audience's consciousness by speeches of the other characters which were designed to contrast his fate with Adam's: thus, at the end of the play, Justice was to warn Adam to 'beware by Lucifer's example of impenitence'. Since the audience's last view of Lucifer would have shown him in his moment of triumph, 'relating, and insulting in what he had done to the destruction of man', the tragedy of *Adam Unparadized* might have been much more open than *Paradise Lost* to the charge of making the devil its hero.

The unusually high proportion of dialogue in *Paradise Lost* may be a reflection of Milton's original dramatic plan, and the angelic chorus which he intended for his tragedy is still part of his epic structure, with its songs punctuating significant moments in the action. The advantages of the change from dramatic to epic form are obvious. Milton is able to involve the reader directly in many things which his concept of tragedy would have obliged him to distance by description. The epic poem had fewer rules to get in his way, and the unique nature of his subject gave him an excuse for breaking many of these. But perhaps the chief advantage was that the story of the fall of man lost its vast collection of allegorical speakers (Justice, Mercy, Conscience, etc.) and acquired one very real one, Milton himself. By making himself so important a character in his poem, he was able both to treat its events from the point of view of a seventeenth-century Christian and, by giving himself an outlet for his own opinions, to allow his characters to speak for themselves. The result is a kind of objectivity that, paradoxically, is essentially dramatic.

Epic and romance

Though Aristotle rated tragedy higher than epic, at the time when Milton wrote *Paradise Lost* it was generally believed that the epic poem was the highest form of literary composition. By epic, critics meant the classical rather than the popular tradition (though, indeed, Homer's poems were recited rather than read), and they knew little about any narratives outside Greek, Latin, and the Romance languages. Pride in their Christian heritage had, however, made them aware of the literary qualities in the Bible; we have seen that Milton called Job a brief epic. Nevertheless, the basic form of narrative which Milton followed is in a direct line from Homer, via Virgil, the sixteenth-century Italian writers, and Spenser. Three separate themes are involved: the Trojan War, the Arthurian legend, and the wars of Charlemagne against the Pagans. But the Trojan story is far the most important of these, and the one from which all the others are derived.

There seems to have been a real event corresponding to the Trojan war, more than a thousand years before the time of Christ. It is thought that by the time Homer's epics were composed this story had already acquired its basic outline, which Homer could take for granted that his audience would know. The *Iliad* and *Odyssey* date from the eighth or seventh century B.C. The first of these tells the story of the war which Greeks and Trojans fought over Helen, a beautiful woman stolen from her Greek husband by Paris, the Trojan prince. More particularly, it is the story of Achilles the Greek hero, who is eventually made to stop sulking in his tent and come out to kill the Trojan champion Hector. The war is still going on when the poem ends, but it is clear that Hector's death will mean the defeat of Troy. In the *Odyssey*, we follow the story of one of the Greek leaders, Odysseus, after the war: it takes him ten years to get home, through many dangers and adventures, and when he does arrive he finds himself having to defeat a band of rival suitors who are courting his wife.

The Homeric epics are good stories not philosophical allegories. But readers since the time of the Romans have liked to find more layers of meaning in them (see Chapter 7 on Myths). Homer's two heroes, Achilles and Odysseus, were taken to be examples of the passionate and the rational man respectively and had a great influence on the characterization of later epic heroes. The war of the *Iliad* and the long journey of the *Odyssey* became the two great epic subjects; both of them were familiar symbols for human life.

The two poems are also a glorification of the Greeks themselves. Many of Homer's original audience may have believed that they were descended from the heroes he described. Naturally, therefore, the hero had to win in the end, and this gave rise to the convention that the epic must always have a happy outcome. But the hero, although invincible, could not be allowed to triumph too easily. An explanation for his failures, weaknesses, and occasional irrational behaviour was provided by the role of the gods in the poem. The hero could hardly be blamed for failing to overcome obstacles put in his way by some capricious and hostile Olympian. What is perhaps most remarkable in Homer is that, although his characters are little more than puppets in the hands of the Olympian gods, they nevertheless leave behind such an impression of courage and vitality.

In the reign of Augustus Caesar, the Roman poet Virgil set out to do for his country what he felt Homer had done for Greece: to celebrate her history, prophesy her future, and provide in his epic hero a character who, like Achilles and Odysseus, could represent a national ideal. He turned to the Trojan story again, but this time from the other side. It was a popular belief, perhaps because a period of migrations and population shifts had followed the historical Trojan War, that the founders of Rome had been Trojans, fleeing after the destruction of their city, who established a new home on Italian soil. The story of Aeneas combines the two Homeric themes of the battle and the voyage; in the first half, the hero and his men make their way to Italy, passing through many trials of which the greatest is Aeneas's love for Dido, Queen of Carthage, and in the second half they have to fight a war before they can be allowed to settle in the new country and intermarry with the local inhabitants. Virgil emphasizes the parallels between his story and Homer's: the Trojan sailors meet some of the same perils as Odysseus; the war in Italy, as in Troy, is fought over a woman; and Turnus, the leader of the Italian army, is referred to as a 'new Achilles'.

Unlike Homer, however, Virgil is not simply telling a good story. His poetic style has a wistfulness that is absent from Homer; his attitude to war is one of horror rather than familiar acceptance; and his portrayal of heroism and triumph is constantly balanced by a sober awareness of what has had to be sacrificed to make them possible. Thus, although Virgil persuades us that Aeneas has to put his divine mission ahead of his love for Dido, he also makes her despairing suicide one of the most tragic moments of the poem. Turnus's hopeless defiance of Aeneas, even though it is against the will of the fates, has a real nobility about it. Despite the capriciousness of the gods as they back first one hero and then another, we are constantly made aware that all this apparent capriciousness is under the control of an overriding power—fate—which it is working to fulfil.

For the events of the *Aeneid* are not merely important in themselves, but also explain later Roman history; for instance, Aeneas's desertion of Dido is the cause of the later enmity between Carthage and Rome. In the sixth book of the poem, Aeneas descends to the underworld, as Homer's Odysseus had done. But whereas Odysseus went there only to cõnsult the prophet Tiresias about the best way to reach his home, Aeneas is told the whole history, up to the time when Virgil wrote, of the empire which he is about to found. Earlier on in the poem, Virgil again follows the *Odyssey* in making Aeneas tell his hosts the events of the earlier part of his journey. But here again the technique contributes to the epic theme. The juxtaposition of Aeneas's account of the fall of Troy with the prophecy of a glorious future for Rome enables Virgil to tell not merely the story of Aeneas himself but also the downfall and rebuilding of an empire. Troy dies and yet it is reborn. The native Italians lose their war with the Trojans and yet it is their name that will be given to the new nation. Perhaps it is this spirit of reconciliation, this muted tone, this sense that 'it's sad, and yet . . .' that is the most Virgilian feature of *Paradise Lost*.

Because most people in western Europe could not read Homer in the original until the Renaissance, it was Virgil who became the model of later epic writers. For at least seventeen hundred years he was held to be the greatest poet who had ever written, and Troy became a symbol for all greatness and majesty which had perished in the past. Other nations also liked to think of themselves as descended from the Trojans. Medieval chroniclers invented a Trojan named Brutus, said to have founded a dynasty in Britain that lasted until the Roman invasion. In the sixth century, chroniclers told of a last-ditch stand against the invading Saxon hordes by a loyal remnant of Britains led by Roman soldiers. Around the name of one of these British heroes, Arthur, there developed, over the next six hundred years, a series of legends which combine Celtic mythology with Christianity. Medieval romances embroidered endlessly on the 'matter of Troy' and 'matter of Britain'. Unlike the epic, these works were primarily about love and magic rather than warfare and patriotism, but the theme of the knightly quest, especially as it appears in the haunting legend of the Holy Grail, recalls the voyage theme of the *Odyssey* and *Aeneid*.

In the sixteenth century the Tudors, who were of Welsh descent, tried to bolster their rather shaky claim to the throne by declaring that Arthur, whose name Henry VII gave to his eldest son, was their ancestor. Writers were encouraged to celebrate this legendary character and treat him seriously as a historical figure. Thus, when Spenser set out at the end of the century to write his allegorical epic in honour of Queen Elizabeth, it was natural for him to turn to the Arthurian material. With characteristic Elizabethan ambition, he planned a structure which, if it had been completed (only about a quarter of it was), would have been longer than the *Iliad*, *Odyssey* and *Aeneid* combined.

The influences which went into the making of *The Faerie Queene*

H

(1596) include the classical epics, the Bible, medieval allegory and chivalric romance, but the work with which Spenser apparently thought of himself as competing was Ariosto's *Orlando Furioso* (published between 1516 and 1532). The Italian epic uses a different story, that of the wars of Charlemagne against the Saracens, which had been the subject of the heroic *Chanson de Roland* in the eleventh or twelfth century. But the highly sophisticated poets Boiardo and Ariosto (whose poem is a sequel to Boiardo's *Orlando Innamorato*) treated their military subject matter with a light touch, combining the romantic colouring of the medieval Arthurian romances with thematic reminiscences of the classical epics. The result was delightful, and Ariosto was responsible for one of the most successful Renaissance works of escape literature; Milton read the conclusion of the *Orlando*, in Harington's 1591 translation, twice in one year, and quoted the poem in his pamphlet *Of Reformation*.

What particularly fascinated Spenser about the Italian epic was its narrative technique. In place of the careful Virgilian epic construction, with its single hero and single action, Ariosto deploys a cast of thousands in a series of elaborately interlocking adventures, often leaving one character in a tight place while he hops over to another episode, and sometimes including, as a sort of bonus, extra stories which the characters tell one another in their rare moments of leisure.

Ariosto was no allegorist, except in a few brief episodes, but allegorical interpretations were foisted onto his work by later critics, as they had been onto those of Homer and Virgil. It was as if readers felt guilty about enjoying a story for its own sake; they were determined to believe that they were being instructed as well. It is in the serious mood of *Il Penseroso*, not the light one of *L'Allegro*, that Milton spends the night reading

> Of tourneys and of trophies hung;
> Of forests, and enchantments drear,
> Where more is meant than meets the ear
> (118–20).

The most curious example of this Renaissance passion for allegorizing is Torquato Tasso. His *Jerusalem Delivered* (1575), the one modern work to which Milton gave the name of epic, tells the story of the First Crusade and the recapture of Jerusalem by the Christians. One might think that such a subject in itself was sufficiently religious and patriotic. But Tasso seems to have felt that he needed to make a claim to a still higher seriousness, by publishing his own interpretation of the poem in which he declared that it was really an allegory of the quest of man (the Christian army) for civil happiness (Jerusalem).

Tasso *was* writing a sort of allegory, though not the one he described. His earthly Jerusalem bears the same relation to the heavenly Jerusalem as Milton's Garden of Eden to the paradise which each man loses when he first loses his innocence. Indeed, the title of Milton's poem may have been suggested to him by Tasso's, which had originally been named after its hero, Godfrey of Boulogne, and then altered, presumably because Tasso realized (did Milton?) that his work had more than one hero. As we have seen, all epic poems were potentially allegorical, in so far as their journeys and battles symbolize a spiritual reality.

But Spenser was the first great writer to use epic material in a directly allegorical way, that is, with a point by point relationship between the events of his literal story and the moral situation which they are supposed to make us understand. And even he is by no means consistently allegorical. At its densest, *The Faerie Queene* works on an astonishing number of levels at once; Duessa in Book I, for instance, stands for falsehood, the Roman Catholic Church, and Mary Queen of Scots. But sometimes the allegory is handled more loosely and leaves room for a large number of purely fanciful stories with only a general relation to the main theme.

One of the chief advantages which Spenser gained from his non-historical, allegorical setting was that it solved the problem of how to handle supernatural characters in a Christian epic. In Homer and Virgil the Olympian gods had provided a useful structural device and an interesting counterpoint between events in heaven and events on earth. But the Christian concept of God was not easily reconciled with this sort of role. For this reason, the Portugese Camoes, in his *Os Lusiadas* (1572), found it easier to build his poem, despite its strongly Christian theme, on a conflict between Venus and Bacchus. Tasso, on the other hand, substituted the angels and devils of his own religion for the Olympian gods; his evil Islamic magicians derive their power from a conventionally grotesque assembly of demons, and the Christians have a celestial army fighting for them. The trouble is that, whereas the rival Olympians are equally balanced, the angels and devils are not; hence, the out-come of the story is a foregone conclusion, and it is hard not to sympathize with the pagan warrior trying to fight a Christian who, unknown to him, is being protected by an invisible angel with a diamond shield. Spenser, however, is able to use figures from the Bible and the classical epic in the same context, because they are all seen in the same allegorical light, that is, as symbols of a higher truth which the resources of ordinary storytelling are inadequate to convey.

The final stage in the transformation of classical into Christian epic may be seen in those seventeenth-century poets who used Spenser's techniques to treat biblical material in a classical way instead of, like him, classical material in a biblical way. Giles Fletcher's *Christ's Victory and Triumph* (1610) is Spenserian to the point of plagiarism sometimes. In his account of the temptation in the wilderness, the characters of Christ and Satan are surrounded by allegorical personifications from the world of the *Faerie Queene*.

Satan himself is described in virtually the same words as Spenser's Archimago, the hypocritical villain who goes about disguised as a pious old man; he leads Christ to such places as the cave of Despair and the palace of Presumption and the lush descriptions of these allegorical settings nearly swamp the story Fletcher is trying to tell.

This is the spirit of Milton's youthful poetry, in which personification (see *The Nativity Ode*, for instance) was obviously second nature to him. His notes for a tragedy, as we have seen, also called for a cast of mainly allegorical characters. But in his epics, apart from the allegorical personifications of Sin, Death, and Chaos, he was writing about 'real' people. The distinction between the real and the allegorical is not easy to make, because epic heroes were generally seen as types anyway. Constant imitation of the Homeric epics had resulted in a remarkable consistency of epic characterization in poets from Virgil to Spenser. Male characters can be pretty well divided into the good leader, the wise old counsellor, the noble adversary, the brave but irrational warrior, and the crafty schemer. The epic is also well supplied with effective portraits of women: the devoted wife, the *femme fatale* (often with magic powers), and the Amazon or woman warrior. The Renaissance epics, because love was nearly as important to them as war, gave a particularly large place to woman, both as temptress and as warrior.

For Milton, who had decided against an Arthurian epic of his own because he had come to doubt the historical validity of the legend, the important thing about the characters of *Paradise Lost* and *Paradise Regained* was that they were *real*. He keeps reminding us of their archetypal nature by such lines as

> Adam the goodliest man of men since born
> His sons, the fairest of her daughters Eve
> > (*PL* IV. 323–4).

As archetypes, they include within themselves all other epic characters. Eve, as Milton portrays her, is both the *femme fatale* and the loyal wife, and Satan embodies all the examples of defiance in a bad cause from Achilles to Tasso's pagan heroes. Comparisons of Satan's followers to the armies described in classical and Italian epic may, as is often suggested, have the effect of deprecating all glorification of military prowess and the old-style epic hero, but the imagery of the poems also associates Adam, Eve, and the Christ of *Paradise Regained* with the idea of spiritual warfare. Eve, like the Lady of *Comus* with her metaphorical armour of chastity, may thus be seen as a woman warrior in the epic tradition, and an example, like Adam and Christ, of

> the better fortitude
> Of patience and heroic martyrdom
> > (*PL* IX. 31–2).

The line that stretches from Spenser's Despair to the Satan of

Paradise Regained illustrates the way in which Milton's archetypes turn allegory inside out. The aged and haggard Despair is one of Spenser's most successful tempters because the lulling rhythm of his verse so perfectly suggests the hypnotic effect he has on his victims. Having already persuaded one young knight to commit suicide, he urges the Redcross Knight to follow this example:

> He there does now enjoy eternal rest
> And happy ease, which thou dost want and crave,
> And farther from it daily wanderest:
> What if some little pain the passage have,
> That makes frail flesh to fear the bitter wave?
> Is not short pain well borne, that brings long ease,
> And lays the soul to sleep in quiet grave?
> Sleep after toil, port after stormy seas,
> Ease after war, death after life, does greatly please.

The toil, stormy seas, and war of the last two lines are all, as we have seen, common images for life. The great temptation for the epic hero is always to stop and rest: Odysseus and Aeneas, in order to carry on their journey, have to desert women who love them and courts where they are feasted and respected. But the rest which Despair offers means death both literally (the Redcross Knight comes very near suicide) and allegorically, since to give up the quest is to be spiritually dead. Milton put an echo of Despair's words into the mouth of Comus, who offers the Lady the cup of intemperance, calling it 'Refreshment after toil, ease after pain'. As in Spenser, the rhythm itself invites her to rest. Adam also, in despair, sees death as a refuge:

> There I should rest
> And sleep secure
> (*PL* X. 778–9).

But at the end of the poem, he and Eve, reconciled to their destiny, begin a new life which is to be both a battle and a journey.

Satan, even more than Adam and Eve, is an exile from his true home, doomed to perpetual restlessness and struggle. When, in *Paradise Regained*, he comes to tempt Christ in the wilderness, he seems at first to be in the same position as Spenser's tempter, offering a weary man inducements to rest at a sumptuous banquet, complete with attendant nymphs and ladies. But most of his temptations in fact are to action; in the scene on the hilltop, he urges Christ to seek glory, empire, and learning. What finally becomes clear is that Christ, unlike all other epic heroes, is a man so completely at peace within himself that neither the supposed duty of action nor the promise of rest has any hold over him. It is Satan himself who has succumbed to the longing for rest. When Christ asks him why he is being urged to assume a kingdom whose coming will mean destruction for the powers of evil, Satan replies,

> Let that come when it comes; all hope is lost
> Of my reception into grace; what worse?
> For where no hope is left, is left no fear;
> If there be worse, the expectation more
> Of worse torments me than the feeling can.
> I would be at the worst; worst is my port,
> My harbour and my ultimate repose,
> The end I would attain, my final good
>   (*PR* III. 204–11).

Spenser's Despair, similarly, though he could tempt others to suicide, longed in vain to die himself. Milton had no need to follow Giles Fletcher's example and have his tempter bring Christ to the cave of Despair, for to say that Satan feels despair, as he does throughout the poem, is also to say that he *is* despair, just as he is also all the other sins that Milton might have personified. With *Paradise Regained*, even more than with *Paradise Lost*, we hit bedrock: we may allegorize the epic themes in terms of our own lives, but if we take Milton's point of view we must say, on the contrary, that our own lives are nothing more than shadowy allegories of his story.

5 Critical analyses

In this Monodie the author bewails a lerned freind unfortunatly drownd in his passage from Chester on the Irish Seas 1637

Yet once more O yee Laurells, and once more
yee myrtles browne wth never sere
I come to pluck yor berries harsh and crude
and wth forc't fingers rude
shatter yor leaves before the mellowing yeare.
bitter constraint and sad occasion deare
compells me to disturbe yor season due
for Lycidas is dead, dead ere his prime
young Lycidas, and hath not left his peere
who would not sing for Lycidas hee well knew
himselfe to sing and built the loftie rime
he must not flote upon his watrie beare
unwept, and welter to the parching wind
without the meed of some melodious teare
Begin then Sisters of the sacred well
that from beneath the seate of Jove doth spring
begin, and somwhat lowdly sweepe the string
hence wth denial vaine, and coy excuse
So may some gentle muse
wth luckie words favour my destin'd urne
and as he passes turne
and bid faire peace be to my sable shroud
for wee were nurst upon the selfe same hill
fed the same flock by fountaine, shade, and rill
Together both ere the high Lawns appear'd
under the opening eyelids of the morne
wee drove afield, and both together heard
what tyme the grey fly winds her sultrie horne
batning our flocks wth the fresh dews of night
oft till the starre that rose in Evning bright
toward heavens descent had sloop't his westring wheele
meane while the rurall ditties were not mute
temper'd to th' oaten flute
rough Satyrs danc't: and Fauns wth cloven heele
from the glad sound would not be absent long
and old Damaetas lov'd to heare our song
But O the heavie change now thou art gone
now thou art gon and never must returne
thee shepheard, thee the woods and desert caves
wth wild Thyme, and the gadding vine oregrowne
and all thir Echos mourne
the willows, and the hazel copses greene
shall now no more be seene
fanning thire joyous leaves to thy soft lays
as killing as the canker to the rose
or taintworme to the weanling heards that graze
or frost to flowrs that thire gay teardrope weares
when first the white thorne blows
such Lycidas thy losse to shepheards eare
where were yee nymphs when ye remorseless deep
clos'd ore the head of yor lov'd Lycidas
for neither were yee playing on the steep
where yor old bards the famous Druids lie
nor on the shaggie top of Mona high
nor yet where Deva spreds her wisard streames
ay mee I fondly dreame
had yee bin there, for what could that have don
what could the golden hayrd Calliope
for her inchaunting son
whome universal nature might lament
when his divine head did
the streame was sent
down the swift Hebrus to
Lesbian shore.

Milton's handwriting, from the ms. in Trinity College, Cambridge

The young Milton, 1625–38

Milton might easily have become a derivative writer. He had been brought up to read and imitate Ovid and Virgil, of whom he was passionately fond; he had a better than average memory; and he seems, especially in his youth, to have known rather less than most people about the world outside books. What saved him was, first, the very number and variety of authors who influenced him, and, second, his unusually strong and stubborn personality.

This personality shows through even in very youthful writings. At seventeen, when he wrote *On the Death of a Fair Infant Dying of the Cough*, a long tradition of allegorizing and Christianizing of classical myth enabled him to move easily from the creation of a myth of his own in the manner of Ovid (Winter, in love with the child, tries to kiss her but accidentally kills her with his icy breath) to a thoroughly Christian conclusion in which the child is seen as an angel interceding for man in heaven. By way of consoling the bereaved mother, the Cambridge freshman then promised that if she bore this loss with patience God would send her another child, presumably a son, 'That to the world's last end shall make thy name to live'. The prospect of fame and immortality probably would not have meant much to a mother at such a time, but there is no doubt that they already meant a great deal to Milton.

Always self-conscious about his poetic development, as he neared the age of twenty-one he made a point of writing poems appropriate to his age—Latin verses on the coming of spring and love at first sight and, possibly, the first of his sonnets, which the editors of the Longman edition tentatively date in the spring of 1629. The writing of love sonnets was traditionally thought of as a young man's pursuit, but it is characteristic of Milton that he should sound rather detached from the whole notion of young love.

Sonnet I

O nightingale, that on yon bloomy spray
    Warblest at eve, when all the woods are still,
    Thou with fresh hope the lover's heart dost fill,
    While the jolly hours lead on propitious May,
5   Thy liquid notes that close the eye of day,
    First heard before the shallow cuckoo's bill
    Portend success in love; O if Jove's will
    Have linked that amorous power to thy soft lay,
Now timely sing, ere the rude bird of hate
10   Foretell my hopeless doom in some grove nigh:
    As thou from year to year hast sung too late
For my relief; yet hadst no reason why,
    Whether the Muse, or Love call thee his mate,
    Both them I serve, and of their train am I.

EXPLANATORY NOTES. It was traditionally believed that to hear the first nightingale of spring before the cuckoo was a good omen to a lover. The cuckoo was a 'bird of hate' not only to lovers but also to husbands because of its association with cuckolding. The nightingale, on the other hand, was supposed originally to have been a ravished maiden named Philomela, who was famous for her sweet singing; hence the bird is associated both with love and with art (the Muse).

CRITICISM. The poet, who has been unlucky in love (or perhaps unlucky in that he has never been in love), begs the nightingale to sing for him, reminding her that as a servant of both Love and the Muses he ought to deserve her kindness. But it is obvious that he only half-believes the superstition he is invoking, since his plea is made only in a conditional sense, 'if' (line 7) she really does have the power to grant it. Even if she does, it is still only by Jove's will— Jove's, not God's, because Milton does not want to overload this secular poem with Christian references, and because the pagan allusion makes the lover's request still more tentative: 'If there *were* a Jove, and if he *did* give such power to the nightingale's song, then . . .'. He is really only playing around with the idea. We are not meant to take the 'bird of hate' too seriously—it is only a 'shallow cuckoo', after all—and still less the poet's 'hopeless doom'. The dominant mood is happy, and the lover's heart is full of hope not merely because the nightingale's song is a good omen and 'propitious May' the month of lovers but also because the season is spring.

VERSIFICATION. Even as a young man Milton preferred to follow the Italian rather than the English examples of the sonnet form. The Elizabethan sonnet made famous by Sidney, Spenser and Shakespeare was composed of three quatrains and a final couplet, and did not have to carry the same rhymes over from one section to the next. The Italian form, often called Petrarchan, falls into an octave and sestet—that is, two quatrains interlinked by rhyme (usually *abba abba*) and six lines which might be rhymed in any one of a variety of ways. The Italian sonnet is difficult to write in English because the language is not very rich in rhymes, but for Milton this technical difficulty only added to the interest of the form. As we shall see, he continued experimenting with it over the next fifteen or twenty years.

Whereas the Elizabethan type of sonnet tends to develop its argument in three stages and then conclude with a neat summing up or surprise twist in the couplet, the Italian one naturally falls into two parts, and it is usually possible to find a transition of some sort at the end of the eighth line. In the case of *Sonnet I*, the octave explains why the poet is addressing the bird and the sestet states what the request is. Yet the break is not made too obvious. For one thing, the entire poem consists of one sentence. For another, although the rhyme scheme changes after line 8, the vowel sounds in 'hate', 'late', and 'mate' connect them with the 'spray', 'May', and so on in the octave.

This concern for structural unity is to be found in all of Milton's major work. He was constantly trying out new devices for holding a poem together: verbal and thematic echoes, carefully placed time references, the disregarding of line and stanza endings, and the use of significant images and myths as a unifying device. His first major poem, written late in 1629 as a birthday present to the infant Christ, shows a surprisingly mature handling of these techniques.

On the Morning of Christ's Nativity, XXIV–XXVII

XXIV

Nor is Osiris seen
In Memphian grove, or green,
    Trampling the unshowered grass with lowings loud:
Nor can he be at rest
Within his sacred chest,
    Nought but profoundest hell can be his shroud,
    In vain with timbrelled anthems dark
The sable-stoled sorcerers bear his worshipped ark.

XXV

He feels from Juda's land
The dreaded infant's hand,
    The rays of Bethlehem blind his dusky eyn;
Nor all the gods beside,
Longer dare abide,
    Not Typhon huge ending in snaky twine:
    Our babe to show his Godhead true,
Can in his swaddling bands control the damned crew.

XXVI

So when the sun in bed,
Curtained with cloudy red,
    Pillows his chin upon an orient wave,
The flocking shadows pale,
Troop to the infernal jail,
    Each fettered ghost slips to his several grave,
And the yellow-skirted fays,
Fly after their night steeds, leaving their moon-loved maze.

XXVII

But see, the virgin blest,
Hath laid her babe to rest.
    Time is our tedious song should here have ending:
Heaven's youngest teemed star,
Hath fixed her polished car,
    Her sleeping Lord with handmaid lamp attending:
And all about the courtly stable,
Bright-harnessed angels sit in order serviceable.

CONTEXT. After dwelling on the peace of the nativity scene and identifying the angelic song heard by the shepherds with the music which accompanied the creation of the world, Milton reminds himself and his reader that this peace and harmony are only temporary; we shall not know them again until the Last Judgment. Nevertheless, Satan is already beginning to feel forebodings of the crushing defeat which Christ will inflict on him then, as the false pagan gods (traditionally identified with the fallen angels) lose their power to deceive mankind.

EXPLANATORY NOTES. Milton is making use of an old tradition that the pagan oracles ceased at the time when Christ was born. The above passage tells how, by his very presence, the child (compared to Hercules, who strangled two serpents while still in his cradle) drives away the gods who take the shape of beasts. Osiris, whose image was carried in a wooden ark, was a bull in appearance, Typhon a monster with a hundred heads, serpent from the waist down. The grass that Osiris treads is 'unshowered' because it is in the hot climate of Egypt, where both these gods were worshipped. 'Eyn' (stanza xxv) is a poetical and archaic word for 'eyes'. Heaven's 'youngest teemed' (newest born) star is the star of Bethlehem which, having guided the Magi to the stable, hovers over it as the poem ends.

CRITICISM. The light-dark contrasts in the *Nativity Ode*, so characteristic of art in the Baroque period, are beautifully handled. The whiteness of the snow and the brightness of the Christ child and angelic choir dominate the first part of the poem, which then modulates, by way of the vision of the Last Judgment, into a mood of darkness and terror. The description of the evil that can only be weakened, not destroyed, by the birth of Christ begins with a dragon (Satan) and ends with the serpent Typhon; their true defeat is still to come. The catalogue of pagan gods proceeds from the more attractive ones—Apollo and the Nymphs, who are pale figures associated with twilight and shadows—to the exotic Ashtaroth who might almost be a statue of the Virgin Mary surrounded with votive candles, and then to the more frightening and evil spirits: Moloch with his 'burning idol all of blackest hue' and the beast-like Egyptian gods, who are given emphatic mention at the end of the list because Egypt was the ancient oppressor of Israel and its religion.

The gloom deepens in stanzas xxiv and xxv, so as to enhance the contrasting brightness of the 'rays of Bethlehem': the priests of Osiris wear black robes; even their anthems are 'dark'; the god himself has 'dusky eyn'. Like the 'shadows pale' of stanza xxvi, who are only reflections of living men, the idols are only feeble likenesses of the true religion. Like the fallen angels in *Paradise Lost*, they are gloomy figures; even at their least malign, they are wistful and somehow sickly. An old and unhealthy religion is being destroyed by the energetic new spirit of Christianity.

Stanza xxvi compares the disappearance of the false gods to the

vanishing of ghosts and fairies at sunrise, but the stanza presents
not only a simile but also a reality: the fairies *are* being banished,
like the other figures already mentioned, though not in so harsh a
way. A similar device, which associates the fairies with evil without
condemning them directly, is found at the end of Book I of *Paradise
Lost*, when the fallen angels, who have reduced themselves to pigmy
size so that they can all get into Pandemonium, are compared to

> faerie elves,
> Whose midnight revels, by a forest side
> Or fountain some belated peasant sees,
> Or dreams he sees, while overhead the moon
> Sits arbitress, and nearer to the earth
> Wheels her pale course
>
> (*PL* I. 781–86).

The red clouds and yellow-skirted fays are the most colourful
images in a poem which otherwise is almost entirely black and white
(the olive green of Peace, the silver chime and age of gold, are
symbolic rather than visual, while both the red fire of Sinai and the
blue furnace of Moloch are dark and smouldering). It is not necessary
to assume that the fays are yellow-skirted only because their modest
author felt they ought to have some clothes on. The yellow colour
associates them first with the sun, whose earliest rays are beginning
to appear, and then with the vanishing moon; unlike the other
shadow figures, they at least enjoy a kind of reflected light.

The image of the sun in bed has sometimes been described as
metaphysical because, unlike the discreet comparisons of the rest
of the poem, it presents its object in a startling and almost comic
way. Its main effect is to provide a transition of both tone and subject, as we move from the dark gods to the light which is chasing
them away, and from the energetic image of Hercules in his cradle
to the reality of the sleeping Christ in his manger. Obviously, the
sun in his baroque, red-curtained bed is not very much like either
of these, but incongruity is inherent in the poem. Christ is both a
child and an epic hero; the scene is a simple, local one, but Christ's
hand reaches from Judah to Egypt; in the last stanza, the phrase
'courtly stable'—that is, the stable which is also a court—neatly
compresses the series of paradoxes.

VERSIFICATION. The final alexandrine (twelve-syllable line) in both
the introductory stanzas and those of the Hymn itself shows Spenser's
influence. There are also characteristic Spenserian archaisms, such
as 'eyn' for 'eyes' in stanza xxv. But the verse form of the Hymn is
that of a traditional carol, and the poem has something of the
naïvety of that genre, occasionally sounding a little awkward in its
self-imposed line lengths ('Nor all the gods beside/ Longer dare
abide', for instance). Punctuation marks at the end of almost every
line invite a more conscious stress on the rhyme than can be found in

most of Milton's later works and even, at times, a rather sing-song delivery in keeping with the style of a carol. But this rhythm can also be dramatically expressive, as in 'Thĕ sáblĕ-stólĕd sorc'rĕrs bĕar hĭs wórshĭpp'd árk', where the Spenserian alliteration of sinister 's' sounds and the regular iambic beat combine to suggest a grisly processional march.

Despite the small scale of the *Nativity Òde*, Milton seems to have approached its composition almost like that of an epic. He uses the device of the angelic song to refer both backward to the Creation and forward to the Last Judgment, thus providing a large framework within which to enclose the single event on which he is concentrating. There is another framework as well, which is equally characteristic of the later Milton: that of the author's presence and participation in the work. Milton makes us see him in the act of writing the poem, eager to present his 'humble ode' to the Christ Child before the Magi arrive with their more splendid offerings. In the last stanza we learn that he has succeeded, and the words 'Time is our tedious song should here have ending' provide a kind of alienation effect by reminding us that what we have just been reading is a very careful piece of composition. It is as if Milton, like some medieval and Renaissance painters, had placed himself among the spectators in the scene he has just portrayed.

His two other poems on Christian festivals, *The Passion* and *The Circumcision*, are less successful attempts to combine the author's experience of a spiritual event with his experience in writing the poem about it. In *The Passion* Milton was never able to get beyond the introductory stanzas: his eyes are on himself all the time, rather than his subject. In an attempt to work himself up to the proper emotions, he falls back on description of his 'pensive trance, and anguish, and ecstatic fit' but fails to convince us that he is feeling any such thing. The poem breaks off as he imagines himself weeping over the sepulchre of Christ, engraving his lines in the rock,

> For sure so well instructed are my tears,
> That they would fitly fall in ordered characters.

After which frigid conceit, he wisely decided that he was not old enough to handle the subject yet.

There is another conceit on tears in *The Circumcision*. Milton behaves here like a stage-manàger addressing his cast: he tells the mourning angels of his scene, who cannot weep because they are made of fire, to 'Burn in your sighs', thus drawing up tears from human mourners to substitute for their own. This idea is sufficiently ingenious to be called metaphysical, as is the pseudo-science of his suggestion, in his comic verses on Hobson's death, that the horse-carrier died during the forced idleness of the vacation because he was 'Made of sphere-metal' and, like the heavenly spheres, immortal so long as he kept moving. Milton's metaphysical conceits really work only in a comic context. His seriousness is not the sort that explodes into fantasy and exaggeration; besides, his natural preference is for a unified effect rather than a series of striking images. In his later works, although some of his images are as unusual as Donne's, he conceals their oddity by a deliberate blurring of the visual aspect—sometimes to the point of producing mixed metaphors which we do not even notice until a critic like Christopher Ricks (in *Milton's Grand Style*) points them out. An exception, perhaps, is the grotesque picture of angelic warfare in *Paradise Lost*, where Raphael, perhaps deliberately, produces at least one image that would have delighted Donne:

> So hills amid the air encountered hills
> Hurled to and fro with jaculation dire,
> That underground they fought in dismal shade
> (VI. 664–6).

Milton the stage-manager is very much present in *L'Allegro* and *Il Penseroso*, but here the charm of the poems results from the perfect blending of the author's mood with the scenes he is describing, so that one cannot say which one causes the other. The goddesses of Mirth and Melancholy are his Muses; when he asks Mirth to bring with her such companions as Jest, Jollity, and Liberty, he is supplying the same sort of stage-directions as when he tells the burning angels of '*The Circumcision*' to weep. The difference is that he makes us *feel* these things instead of just telling us that they are there.

L'Allegro, 91–116

Sometimes with secure delight
The upland hamlets will invite,
When the merry bells ring round,
And the jocund rebecks sound
95   To many a youth, and many a maid,
Dancing in the chequered shade;
And young and old come forth to play
On a sunshine holiday,
Till the livelong daylight fail,
100   Then to the spicy nut-brown ale,
With stories told of many a feat,
How Faëry Mab the junkets eat,
She was pinched, and pulled she said,
And by the friar's lantern led
105   Tells how the drudging goblin sweat,
To earn his cream-bowl duly set,
When in one night, ere glimpse of morn,
His shadowy flail hath threshed the corn,
That ten day-labourers could not end;
110   Then lies him down the lubber fiend.

And stretched out all the chimney's length,
Basks at the fire his hairy strength;
And crop-full out of doors he flings,
Ere the first cock his matin rings.

115 Thus done the tales, to bed they creep,
By whispering winds soon lulled asleep.

CONTEXT. This account of how L'Allegro (the cheerful man) spends the afternoon comes between the account of his morning rambles in the country and the more refined pleasures of tournaments, plays and music in which he passes the evening.

EXPLANATORY NOTES. 'Secure' means carefree, 'rebecks' are fiddles, 'junkets' are foods made from cream, of which the fairies were supposed to be particularly fond. The 'friar' of line 104 is probably an alternate name for Robin Goodfellow, the goblin, who was thought to lead people astray like a will-o'-the-wisp.

CRITICISM. It is curious, but characteristic of the bookish young Milton, that more than half this description of a country holiday should be taken up with the stories told by the rustics after the dance is done. Similarly, in the final section of the poem, L'Allegro supposedly goes to seek 'the busy hum of men', but mixes with them only as a spectator at tournament or theatre. Like Il Penseroso, he is really a solitary figure.

As in *Sonnet I* and the *Nativity Ode*, Milton makes use of folklore without committing himself to belief in it. Here it is all put into the mouths of simple country people and the various terms applied to Robin Goodfellow nicely catch the ambivalent attitude of the speakers toward this helpful goblin: he is a 'fiend', and his 'shadowy flail' might be sinister in another context, yet he is faintly ridiculous too—'drudging', 'lubber', sweating for his reward, and finally 'crop-full' of cream.

The gaiety of the first part of the passage and the excited speech of the characters in the latter part are conveyed by the equally breathless syntax and punctuation. It is not at all clear whether the two lines immediately preceding this extract,

Or if the earlier season lead
To the tanned haycock in the mead,

are meant to go with the previous description of Phillis and Thestylis or with L'Allegro's visit to the upland hamlets. This kind of uncertainty is frequent. Line 98, for example, looks like the end of the sentence but is not; on the other hand, the full-stop after line 110 is a surprise. Lines 102–105 are hard to follow either logically or grammatically. Yet none of this seems to matter. It is perfectly easy to know what is going on. There is nothing either witty or funny about the passage and yet it communicates a tremendous sense of pleasure, liveliness, gaiety.

VERSIFICATION. The basic metre is the octasyllabic (eight-syllable) couplet, popular with Chaucer and the Elizabethans for just this sort of light-toned narrative. It is freely varied (for instance, three out of the first four lines have only seven syllables) and requires frequent use of elision to make some of the lines scan. This, of course, adds to the speed of the rhythm, and the many variations from iambic to trochaic (that is, from ˘ ‾ to ‾ ˘) give it a tripping effect. Seventeenth-century punctuation tends to be, from our point of view, rather light; it often uses commas where we should want a full stop. In prose as well as verse it is easy to find sentences of the type Milton has written here, running on and on with the aid of connecting words like 'after', 'when', 'until', 'then', and so on. Though the sentence structure in *Il Penseroso* is similar, the movement of the poem is slower and the transitions are easier to follow. It may be significant that 'the mountain nymph, sweet Liberty' is invoked only in *L'Allegro*, since Liberty includes freedom to experiment with the conventions of verse form. Milton tells Mirth to 'trip it as you go' and Melancholy to come 'With even step, and musing gait', and the two poems live up to his instructions.

Milton's attitude towards the fairy tales and mythology which fill his early writings is perhaps best summed up in the words of the Attendant Spirit in *Comus*, his next major work:

> I'll tell ye, 'tis not vain or fabulous,
> (Though so esteemed by shallow ignorance)
> What the sage poets taught by the heavenly Muse,
> Storied of old in high immortal verse
> Of dire chimeras and enchanted isles,
> And rifted rocks whose entrance leads to hell,
> For such there be, but unbelief is blind
>
> (512–18).

There were, as we have already seen, many ways in which a Christian poet could make use of this 'fabulous' material without going against his duty to speak the truth. He could handle it in a light, half-sceptical manner, as in *Sonnet I*, treat it as an antagonist to the true faith, as in the *Nativity Ode*, or simply enjoy it on the level of fantasy, as in *L'Allegro*, where the essential innocence of the rustics who believe in fairies is shown by the ease with which they fall asleep at the end of their story-telling.

Comus, like the early poem *On the Death of a Fair Infant*, uses supernatural pagan figures in a Christian context, but instead of making an easy transition from myth to religion as he had done before Milton deliberately emphasizes the moment at which they cease to be interchangeable. At first sight it seems simple enough to take the masque as an allegory of the Circe myth in which the three children lost in the woods are simultaneously involved, on the one hand, with a fairytale enchanter, a messenger of the gods, and a water spirit, and, on the other, with a struggle against sensuality and intemperance. But in fact Milton is dealing with two different worlds. Some of his characters are able to move from one to the other. The Attendant Spirit, who describes himself as a Platonic *daemon* from the moon, seems also to be a Christian guardian angel; hence the irony of the Elder Brother's words to him: 'I'll follow thee, And some good angel bear a shield before us' (657). Sabrina seems likewise to be both a water nymph and a symbol of divine grace. But the Egerton children, since they play themselves in the masque, never cease to be Christians. Comus, on the other hand, is pagan throughout. The result is a clash of cultures, which becomes particularly apparent in the central confrontation between the Lady and Comus.

Comus, 778–798

Lady.   . . . Shall I go on?
Or have I said enough? To him that dares
780   Arm his profane tongue with contemptuous words
Against the sun-clad power of chastity;
Fain would I something say, yet to what end?
Thou hast nor ear, nor soul to apprehend
The sublime notion, and high mystery
785   That must be uttered to unfold the sage
And serious doctrine of virginity,
And thou art worthy that thou shouldst not know
More happiness than this thy present lot.
Enjoy your dear wit, and gay rhetoric
790   That hath so well been taught her dazzling fence,
Thou art not fit to hear thyself convinced;
Yet should I try, the uncontrolled worth
Of this pure cause would kindle my rapt spirits
To such a flame of sacred vehemence,
795   That dumb things would be moved to sympathize,
And the brute Earth would lend her nerves, and shake,
Till all thy magic structures reared so high,
Were shattered into heaps o'er thy false head.

CONTEXT.   This is the Lady's reply to the most gorgeous speech in the play, Comus's attempt to persuade her that the bounty of Nature is a sign that abstinence is displeasing to God (or rather, to 'the all-giver', since Milton is careful not to give the pagan Comus any specifically Christian expressions). She has begun by trying to reply on the level of practical common sense and natural reason—Comus's own ground—arguing that the example of Nature ought to teach man temperance rather than gluttony. Then she breaks off, refusing to tell him any more. The effect of the above lines, the last which the Lady speaks in the masque, is to make Comus feel a 'cold shuddering dew' all over him. He manages nevertheless to dissemble and renew his attack, until her brothers enter to drive him and his crew away.

CRITICISM. Despite their impact on Comus, the Lady's words have often been taken as a confession of failure on Milton's part or hers. Why *doesn't* she go on to explain the 'doctrine of virginity'? Is this a case, like Samson's 'rousing motions', of a kind of spiritual experience which is incommunicable and therefore undramatic?

There seems to be two reasons why the Lady cannot answer. The first is the one she gives: Comus has 'nor ear, nor soul to apprehend' what she wants to say. The son of Circe and Bacchus is not part of the same spiritual world as his antagonist. He understands her no more than Caliban in *The Tempest* understands Miranda. The Attendant Spirit has said, of the followers of Comus, that after their transformation into beasts they,

> so perfect is their misery,
> Not once perceive their foul disfigurement,
> But boast themselves more comely than before
>
> (73–5).

Because they are happy in their brutishness, they cannot be restored to their human shape, as usually happens in versions of the Circe myth. In the same way, Comus thinks himself happy, although from the point of view of the Lady and the Attendant Spirit not to know 'more happiness than this thy present lot' is to be wretched. The Lady hates to give Comus the satisfaction of remaining unanswered, but she can see that to reply would be a waste of time.

But if she were to reply, what would she say? The 'sage/ And serious doctrine of virginity' was not one which could be proclaimed in the context of a masque, for, unlike the classical virtues of chastity and temperance which Comus is attacking, it is part of Christian belief. We know from the *Apology for Smectymnuus* that Milton had been much impressed in his youth by the 'chaste and high mysteries' of such scriptural passages as the description in Revelation of the saints who follow the Lamb: 'These are they which were not defiled with women, for they are virgins' (Rev. 14:4). He adds that 'marriage must not be called a defilement', thus agreeing with Spenser (to whom he applied the words 'sage and serious' in *Areopagitica*) whose *Faerie Queene* presents a Lady Knight, Britomart, both as the defender of chastity and as the destined bride of Artegall (Justice). In the Attendant Spirit's final speech we see that the ideal couple Cupid and Psyche are to have children according to Jove's promise. The Lady's concept of virginity, then, is mystical rather than physical, and cannot be conveyed in words even to believers. It is the 'unexpressive [i.e. inexpressible] nuptial song' of *Lycidas*, and the 'beatitude past utterance' which the angels in *Paradise Lost* receive from the sight of God (III. 62).

Though the Lady's speech is a refusal to do verbal battle, its imagery is almost entirely military. Comus is said to 'arm his profane tongue' against Chastity in her shining armour (like Britomart's), his eloquent arguments are compared to the art of fencing, and the Lady's words, if she allowed herself to speak them, would be capable of bringing down Comus's palace. But this is not to happen. Similarly, when the brothers rush in with their drawn swords, there is no real battle. Comus and his rout 'make signs of resistance but are all driven in'. Evil cannot be finally captured or defeated in this work. The children may 'triumph' over the temptation to 'sensual folly and intemperance' in themselves, but they cannot remove it from the world.

VERSIFICATION. Milton's blank verse is more regular than that of the dramatists with whom he was contemporary, and thus close to that of the early Shakespeare. Occasional *feminine endings* (in which the stress does not fall on the final syllable of a line) are his main kind of variation; for instance, earlier in the Lady's speech, 'Imposter do not charge most innocent Nature'. But in the above extract, where the Lady is quite sure of what she is saying, the even stress of the lines gives an extra sharpness to her tone which no doubt adds to its devastating effect on Comus.

Though *Comus* is often described as being more of a poem than a drama, there is no doubt that the dramatic form helped Milton to deal with the problem of relating his feelings as an artist to the feelings called for by his subject matter. It also gave him freedom to explore poetic themes which he could not have handled in his own person as a poet. Comus's entrance speech, for instance, is in the metre and manner of *L'Allegro* and *Il Penseroso*:

> Meanwhile, welcome joy, and feast,
> Midnight shout, and revelry,
> Tipsy dance, and jollity
>
> (102–4).

But his creation of this devil's advocate allowed Milton to write about revels L'Allegro would never have approved and nocturnal pleasures unknown to Il Penseroso, safe in the knowledge that they were all ultimately to be rejected.

The masque, which required the welding together of speech, music, and spectacle, was Milton's most ambitious and large-scale achievement of unity within diversity. But it was in the superficially much simpler form of the pastoral that he wrote the most complex of all his early works. *Lycidas* is a dramatic poem, with a surprising amount and variety of direct speech; like *Comus*, though with greater control, it uses pagan mythology for the allegorical expression of Christian truth, finally discarding the myth when it has done all it can do. Despite its variety of tone (partly indicated by Milton's own stage directions: 'Begin, and somewhat loudly sweep the string', 'That strain I heard was of a higher mood', 'return Sicilian muse'), the poem is held together by a network of elaborately interconnecting images and by the alternation of anguished questions with only partially satisfactory answers until the final lines which resolve all discords through faith.

Lycidas, 1–14

Yet once more, O ye laurels, and once more
Ye myrtles brown, with ivy never sere,
I come to pluck your berries harsh and crude,
And with forced fingers rude,
5   Shatter your leaves before the mellowing year.
Bitter constraint, and sad occasion dear,
Compels me to disturb your season due:
For Lycidas is dead, dead ere his prime,
Young Lycidas, and hath not left his peer:
10   Who would not sing for Lycidas? he knew
Himself to sing, and build the lofty rhyme.
He must not float upon his watery bier
Unwept, and welter to the parching wind,
Without the meed of some melodious tear.

EXPLANATORY NOTES.   Lycidas, a pastoral name found in Theocritus and Virgil among others, is Edward King, who was shipwrecked and drowned in the Irish Sea at the age of twenty-five. Milton's poem was the last one in the memorial volume of verses by King's Cambridge acquaintances; in all, there were twenty-three poems in Latin and Greek and thirteen in English.

CRITICISM.   Collections such as the one to which Milton was contributing were often called 'garlands', 'songs', or 'tears'. In the first lines of his elegy Milton uses all three of these descriptions of what he is about to do. The speaker is plucking laurels, myrtles and ivy to make a garland for the dead poet. But the berries of these plants are harsh and crude; it is too soon to gather them, not only because they are not yet ready, but also because the speaker himself is not: his fingers are clumsy. Yet Lycidas, like the plants, has been gathered before his prime, and thus it is appropriate that he should have his 'song' from another young poet, however immature.

Just as he offers an unripe garland to an untimely death and a song to a singer, so Milton, in the last three lines of this extract, gives a further, and at first sight a curious, reason why his poem will be appropriate to the situation. King has died by drowning, and therefore he must have a 'melodious tear'. The idea would be almost ludicrous, like the conceits on tears in *The Passion* and *On the Circumcision*, except that the word 'melodious' neutralizes any possible visual impression of the tear.

The connection between death by drowning and the tears of the mourners is a common one, and inspired several of the other poets who contributed to the Edward King miscellany. One of them, the metaphysical John Cleveland, found a more ingenious conceit on the subject:

> I am no poet here; my pen's the spout
> Where the rain-water of my eyes runs out
> In pity of that name, whose fate we see
> Thus copied out in grief's hydrography.

That is, Cleveland is weeping so much that he can actually write with his tears ('hydrography'—water-writing—is a characteristic metaphysical coinage). The idea is grotesque and is meant to be so. Cleveland's poem consists entirely of such conceits as this, held together simply by the writer's personality.

In *Lycidas*, on the other hand, the individual conceit of shedding tears for a drowned man is subordinated to the total poetic pattern. We do not really understand why the body in the Irish sea should be described as if it were being dried out by the 'parching wind' until we have been led through the different water images of the poem—the fountains and rivers of pastoral literature, the river Hebrus, the sea of Galilee, the metaphorical sea of the voyage through life (the 'perilous flood' of line 185 surely means this as well as the Irish sea)—to the truly healing waters which are the 'other groves, and other streams' of heaven (line 174). Yet this ingenuity of imagery and structure does not draw attention to itself. It is characteristic of classical poetry that the whole should be greater than the sum of its parts.

VERSIFICATION. The verse form of *Lycidas* is uncommon in English; it consists of verse paragraphs of irregular length, each of which concludes with a couplet. The lines are also of uneven length; they nearly always rhyme, but in an irregular manner. In Italian this type of poem is much commoner. It is called a *canzone* (literally, song), and its irregular form is meant to suggest the spontaneity of the inspired singer. Petrarch was one of many writers who used it skilfully.

The complexity of the versification varies throughout the poem to mirror the state of the poet's thoughts. In this respect, it can be compared with some metaphysical lyrics—for example, George Herbert's *Denial*, which in its first five stanzas uses a deliberately awkward verse form and unrhymed final line to re-enact the poet's sense of disjointedness when he thinks himself abandoned by God; in the last stanza, the poet smoothes out the verse and lets the rhymes fall into place, thus indicating the harmony which God can restore to his life. A similar transition occurs in lines 165–85 of Milton's elegy, beginning,

> Weep no more, woeful shepherds weep no more,
> For Lycidas your sorrow is not dead.

This is a subtler version of the same device that has already been noted in Spenser's *November Eclogue* (see p. 87), the change from a tragic to a joyous refrain. But the cadence of line 165 not only echoes the first line of the poem, 'Yet once more, O ye laurels, and once more', it also resolves it: for that first line is one of the ten unrhymed ones which Milton left in *Lycidas* to symbolize the discord of the speaker's mind and to contrast with the final section in which everything does rhyme.

The metre which Milton chose for the very end—'Thus sang the uncouth swain', etc.—is *ottava rima* (an eight-line stanza rhyming *abababcc*). It may be significant, in view of the fact that the swain seems to be leaving the pastoral world behind him, that in Italian poetry *ottava rima* was the normal verse form for the epic.

The years of revolution, 1639–60

We know that Milton came back from Italy determined to write a masterpiece to the glory of England and that he spent most of the next twenty years doing other things instead. It used to be thought that his three major works dated from after the Restoration, which is when they were published. Now it seems that only *Paradise Regained* was composed entirely after 1660. *Paradise Lost* was probably begun in the last years of the Commonwealth, and some dramatic fragments may have been worked into it from still earlier drafts. *Samson Agonistes* has always been a puzzle to date: traditionally it has been thought of as belonging to a period after Milton had lost both his eyesight and his hopes of a free Commonwealth, but many modern scholars, including his biographer W. R. Parker, now argue for a much earlier date, possibly even before Milton's blindness. Their reasons are mainly stylistic: Milton uses rhyme in the Choruses but had discarded it for large-scale works by the time he began *Paradise Lost;* the Choruses, moreover, resemble other metrical experiments of the 1640s and early 50s, such as his psalm translations.

It seems curious, in that case, that he did not publish his tragedy until after the Restoration. Perhaps, with the onset of blindness, he found that it had become too personal a work and one which might give the Royalist pamphleteers of the 1650s a weapon to use against him; one can imagine them quoting lines out of context to prove that Milton knew himself justly punished for rebelling against his king. He had himself done the same sort of thing in his dispute with Bishop Hall, quoting and ridiculing his adversary's early satiric poems. In 1671 it could make no difference what people said. He published his Old Testament tragedy in the same volume with his

New Testament epic, *Paradise Regained*, as if to encourage his readers to notice the contrast between the two different kinds of redeemers.

No matter when we date *Samson Agonistes*, it stands in striking contrast to Milton's other works. Its dramatic form does not make for variety, as in *Comus;* even *Lycidas*, where the conflicts are all within one character, balances light and shade in a way that this tragedy does not. In his search for tragic unity, he has pared down his materials rather than seeking to reconcile their differences; in strict decorum to his biblical story, he has also cut out the extra dimension which classical references and allegory gave to his earlier work. What he gains is intensity, but of a peculiarly painful kind.

Samson Agonistes, 1669–1707

Semichorus. While their hearts were jocund and sublime,

1670 Drunk with idolatry, drunk with wine
And fat regorged of bulls and goats,
Chanting their idol, and preferring
Before our living dread who dwells
In Silo his bright sanctuary:

1675 Among them he a spirit of frenzy sent,
Who hurt their minds,
And urged them on with mad desire
To call in haste for their destroyer;
They only set on sport and play

1680 Unweetingly importuned
Their own destruction to come speedy upon them.
So fond are mortal men
Fallen into wrath divine,
As their own ruin on themselves to invite,

1685 Insensate left, or to sense reprobate,
And with blindness internal struck.
Semichorus. But he though blind of sight,
Despised and thought extinguished quite,
With inward eyes illuminated

1690 His fiery virtue roused
From under ashes into sudden flame,
And as an evening dragon came,
Assailant on the perched roosts,
And nests in order ranged

1695 Of tame villatic fowl; but as an eagle
His cloudless thunder bolted on their heads.
So virtue given for lost,
Depressed, and overthrown, as seemed,
Like that self-begotten bird

1700 In the Arabian woods embossed,
That no second knows nor third,
And lay erewhile a holocaust,

From out her ashy womb now teemed,
Revives, reflourishes, then vigorous most
1705   When most unactive deemed,
And through her body die, her fame survives,
A secular bird ages of lives.

CONTEXT. Having just heard the messenger describe how Samson
destroyed himself and the Philistines together, the Chorus rejoice
in his 'dearly-bought revenge, yet glorious'. Milton splits them into
two groups; the first *semichorus* (or half-chorus) sings of the mad
blindness which God inflicted on the Philistines, making them call
for their own ruin in the person of Samson, while the second group
contrasts this with the inner light, also sent from God, which enabled the seemingly blind Samson to become a minister of vengeance.

EXPLANATORY NOTES. 'Sublime' means lifted up and is not a term
of praise. Silo (Shiloh) was where the Ark of the Covenant was kept
in Israel. In line 1670, 'fat', like 'drunk' in the previous line, refers
to the Philistines, who have been gorging themselves on meat;
'regorged' conveys the idea of excess, and goat's meat was forbidden
to the Israelites, so there is an extra touch of disgust and self-
righteousness in the Chorus's mention of this detail. 'Dragon' (line
1692) means snake, and 'villatic' is Milton's way of avoiding the
more prosaic adjective 'farmyard'. The thunder is cloudless because
it is divine rather than natural and thus gives no warning of its
coming. The 'self-begotten bird' of line 1699 is the mythical Phoenix
of Arabia, of which there was never more than one in the world at
a time because it died ('embossed', or sheltered, in the woods) by
burning to death in its nest and then rose from its own ashes. It is
thus 'a secular bird ages of lives'—that is, it lives forever, but in
many different lives.

CRITICISM. There are times when, in reading *Samson*, one is inclined to agree with Northrop Frye's description of the Chorus,
'standing around uttering timid complacencies in teeth-loosening
doggerel'. They have already shown their timidity earlier in this
scene when, hearing a crash and screams offstage, they decide not
to investigate but to wait until someone comes along to tell them
what has happened. However, this unlikely behaviour (which is
common in classical choruses) is really only a technical device for
preserving unity of place and allowing the important news to be
told in front of the audience. There is nothing timid in their response
to the messenger, which is one of unholy glee at the destruction of
their enemies (it is hard to see why Manoa follows this triumphant
outburst with 'Come, come, no time for lamentation now').

The behaviour of the Philistines, as described in the first semichorus, corresponds to the Greek concept of *hubris*—the arrogance
in relation to the gods that was supposed to lead to man's downfall.
The second semichorus parallels this with the case of Samson, who

is described in terms both of a natural, irrational force (a snake or eagle) and of a vehicle of divine power, which takes the form of fire. Samson himself had said that

> cords to me were threads
> Touched with the flame
> (261–2).

—that is, that the spirit of God within him was like a fire and made him invincible. The image of his rising from his own ashes like the Phoenix is thus associated with the reappearance of this divine inspiration. But the animal imagery (even if Milton does try to elevate his picture of a snake raiding a chicken coop by the almost comically elaborate diction of lines 1692–5) makes us aware of the barbaric and even frightening aspect of Samson's character. The Phoenix comparison associates Samson with .Christ, of whose resurrection the bird was thought to be a symbol, but the comparison is also a contrast. Samson himself is promised only the immortality of fame, not that of a life after death.

VERSIFICATION. How exactly Milton intended the choruses in *Samson* to be scanned has never been satisfactorily explained. His metre is irregular, with occasional rhymes at unpredictable intervals and no discernable stanzaic or metrical pattern; there is no 'norm', as in the eight-syllable line of *L'Allegro* or the iambic pentameter of *Paradise Lost*, against which to measure deviations. All one can do is to read the lines aloud with the normal stress that one would give them in prose; where this plainly will not do, as in line 1684 ('As their own ruin on themselves to invite'), other ways must be tried. In this particular case, the easiest solution is to make the elision between the last two words, so that the line becomes an ordinary blank verse one:

> As théir ówn ruin on themsélves t'invíte.

The stress on 'their own' is important for the meaning of the line. Line 1682 is probably better scanned

> Só fónd are mórtal mén

rather than the alternative

> So fónd are mórtal mén,

because the extra stress on 'so' is more expressive of the Chorus's tone of satisfaction and wonder. But there is no certain way of saying which is right.

Apart from the word 'invite' (line 1684), which helps provide a bridge between the two semichoruses, there are no obvious rhyme words in the first part of the extract. But there are several examples of something which certainly would be called assonance, or half-rhyme, if it occurred in the work of a twentieth-century poet:

'sublime/wine', 'desire/destroyer', 'them/men', 'invite/reprobate'. It would be interesting to know whether these were intentional or simply, like the occasional rhymes in *Paradise Lost*, the result of an unconscious attraction to sound-patterning.

The unusual technical features of Milton's choruses have made them of special interest to modern poets—Hopkins and Eliot, for example—who, like him, have tried to find new rhythms for the language of poetry. Though he seems to have written them with no intention of their being set to music, they sometimes fall into a syncopated beat which suggests a chant rather than naturalistic speech, and for which the closest modern alternative would be the poetry that is written to be recited with a jazz accompaniment.

Perhaps the brevity of the sonnet form was one reason for Milton's attraction to it during the 1640s and 50s. While he was still active politically, it was something he could do during his few spare moments; after his blindness, he may have found it easiest at first to retain only a few lines in his head at once.

Apart from the early *Sonnet I*, 'O Nightingale', and his Italian sequence, Milton's sonnets differ from those of the Elizabethans in not being about love. His precedents were the 'heroic sonnets' which Tasso addressed to public figures of his own time and the dedicatory sonnets which Spenser, at the beginning of the *Faerie Queene*, addressed to members of Queen Elizabeth's court. The tone of these middle-period sonnets is mature, at times almost avuncular, and moralistic. Most are addressed to people he admired or liked; a few are personal and autobiographical; others might be described as political.

They show a remarkable range. The wittiest are the satirical ones, which make clever use of proper names in key positions, comic rhymes, and run-on lines that go against the natural texture of the poem—for instance, in his picture of puzzled passers-by gazing at the mysterious title *Tetrachordon* on the outside of one of his divorce tracts:

> Cries the stall-reader, Bless us! what a word on
> A title-page is this! And some in file
> Stand spelling false, while one might walk to Mile-
> End Green. Why is it harder sirs than Gordon,
> Colkitto, or Macdonnel, or Galasp?
>
> *(Sonnet XI.)*

To prove that there is nothing extraordinary in his polysyllabic title, he produces three other words that rhyme with it.

The sonnets of friendship and praise are often described as Horatian. We have seen that Horace, the poet of the good life, the quiet happiness, the moderate virtues, was an inspiration to some seventeenth-century poets whose attitude to the good life was considerably less restrained than his. Temperance, however, was a congenial theme to Milton and in *Sonnets XVII* and *XVIII* he strikes a careful balance between excess and abstinence: young Lawrence is told that it is wise to be able to enjoy good things in moderation, while Skinner is warned that, though it may seem wise to fill one's day with business and study, it is not God's will that men should never take pleasure in life when it lies ready to hand. One wonders, though, what Skinner thought when he read the jolly-sounding invitation, 'Today deep thoughts resolve with me to drench', and then found in the next line not wine but 'In mirth, that after no repenting draws'. Perhaps the comic anticlimax was intentional.

Sonnet XVII

Lawrence of virtuous father virtuous son,
   Now that the fields are dank, and ways are mire,
   Where shall we sometimes meet, and by the fire
   Help waste a sullen day; what may be won
5 From the hard season gaining: time will run
   On smoother, till Favonius reinspire
   The frozen earth; and clothe in fresh attire
   The lily and rose, that neither sowed nor spun.
What neat repast shall feast us, light and choice,
10 Of Attic taste, with wine, whence we may rise
   To hear the lute well touched, or artful voice
Warble immortal notes and Tuscan air?
   He who of those delights can judge, and spare
   To interpose them oft, is not unwise.

EXPLANATORY NOTES. See p. 163 for short biography of Lawrence. The theme of enjoying oneself indoors on a cold wintry day is a Horatian one, and some of the poem's references are classical. Favonius is the Latin name for the west wind, associated with spring; a meal of Attic taste would, literally, be Greek, but in this context means a refined and frugal one. The Tuscan airs could be classical, but it is more likely that Milton was thinking of a musical setting of one of his favourite Italian poets.

CRITICISM. This sonnet has sometimes been described as an invitation to supper—a common Horatian theme which Ben Jonson handled memorably in his poem *Inviting a Friend to Supper*—but in fact it does not tell Lawrence when and where to come, only asks him to consider the idea in the abstract, perhaps as an alternative to taking walks now that the weather has made these impossible. Milton asks, rather than says, what they shall have to eat, and is similarly indecisive about the music to follow; the result is that our picture of the proposed meal is tantalizingly vague, which is suitable for a poem on temperate enjoyment, since it ought not to be overloaded with indigestible descriptions of food and drink.

The last two lines, perhaps unintentionally, add to the ambiguity surrounding the whole treatment of pleasure in this sonnet. The words 'judge' and 'spare' can be taken two ways. Is Milton saying that it is wise to judge just how little the delights of food, wine and music are worth and refrain from enjoying them too often, or does he mean that one should be discriminating enough to enjoy these tastes and sensible enough to spare the time to indulge them? The word 'interpose' suggests that perhaps the question is irrelevant. Milton is obviously not thinking of making every day an occasion for feasting. Both he and Lawrence have other things to do, and he knows it.

But there is a further level to the poem, which goes beyond Horace as, in *Comus*, the Lady's doctrine of virginity goes beyond the rest of the masque. Milton is writing about a time of year when winter is coming on ('the hard season' is 'gaining') and looking forward to the return of spring which will breathe new life into ('reinspire') the frozen earth. This imagery, suggesting the idea of resurrection, is followed by the reference to Christ's parable of the lilies who 'toil not, neither do they spin', but are nevertheless clothed by God. For Milton the parable is not an excuse for idleness; Christ goes on to ask why, since God can take care even of such perishable things as flowers, 'shall he not much more clothe you, O ye of little faith?' (Matthew 6:28–30). It is through his faith and trust in God that man can afford to be merry even in the winter, knowing that the spring will come again.

VERSIFICATION. Though he makes a break between octave and sestet, Milton's use of the sonnet form here is otherwise freer than in *Sonnet I*. The pauses, except at the end of line 8, are placed so as to prevent the voice from resting on rhyme words, and thus the octave can be read as a single sentence, with emphasis falling on the crucial line about the lily and rose. The rhyming of the sestet (*cdceed*) is somewhat unusual too, and the last two lines of the poem, where the moral is stated, are separated from the rest almost like the final couplet of an Elizabethan sonnet.

As Milton arranged his sonnets in the 1673 edition of his poems, the above lines to Edward Lawrence actually followed the sonnet on the Piedmontese massacre and the famous one on his blindness, which came between them. Recent editors of the sonnets think that this order was thematic rather than chronological, designed to show a progression of the poet's mood from the violence of his cry for vengeance on the perpetrators of the massacre, through the impatience and gradual resignation of his attitude to his personal suffering, to the tranquillity and cheerfulness of his invitation to enjoy the pleasures of life. *Sonnet XV* was probably not written much later than *XVII* in any case, but it strikingly anticipates the manner of Milton's later works.

Avenge O Lord thy slaughtered saints, whose bones
Lie scattered on the Alpine mountains cold,
Even them who kept thy truth so pure of old
When all our fathers worshipped stocks and stones,
5   Forget not: in thy book record their groans
Who were thy sheep and in their ancient fold
Slain by the bloody Piedmontese that rolled
Mother with infant down the rocks. Their moans
The vales redoubled to the hills, and they
10   To heaven. Their martyred blood and ashes sow
O'er all the Italian fields where still doth sway
The triple Tyrant: that from these may grow
A hundredfold, who having learnt thy way
Early may fly the Babylonian woe.

EXPLANATORY NOTES. We have already seen (p. 62) that the massacre of the Vaudois in 1655 brought cries of outrage from the Protestant nations of Europe, led by England. The Vaudois, who inhabited a few small Alpine villages on the Franco-Italian border, had been separated from the Church of Rome since 1215. They were thus regarded by English Protestants as among the first of the 'saints' to make war on the 'Whore of Babylon'—to use the language which they borrowed from the Book of Revelation—at a time when the rest of Europe was still practising the idolatries of Rome to which Milton refers in line 4. Savoy was the 'ancient fold' of the Vaudois because they had been granted the right to reside there since 1561. Milton's sonnet echoes the language of the letters which he sent in Cromwell's name to other Protestant countries, and also that of contemporary news-letters describing the massacre.

CRITICISM. 'The blood of the martyrs is the seed of the Church.' This is one of several metaphors which Milton's imagination has fused in this extremely rapid and condensed poem; others are the myth of the dragon's teeth sown by Cadmus which sprang up as armed men and the biblical lament 'our bones are scattered at the grave's mouth'. There is also, in the reference to the Vaudois as sheep in their 'ancient fold', a kind of grisly pastoral image. Cromwell had at one point thought of sending an army into Savoy, but it seems that Milton thinks of the blood and ashes of the martyrs as giving life, not to soldiers, but to new converts to the true faith. His cry for vengeance rises to God alone.

VERSIFICATION. It is difficult, and this is typical of Milton's poetry from this point on, to separate discussion of the poem from analysis of the verse techniques by which Milton achieves its majestic and immensely solemn forward movement. The passionate feeling behind his writing, and perhaps also the image of victims being hurled over a precipice, led him to disregard line and stanza endings to an extent unprecedented in either his own work or that of the Italian sonneteers. This enables him, as later in *Paradise Lost*, to put special stress on key words at the beginnings of lines: 'Forget not', 'To heaven', and 'The Triple Tyrant', for example. The movement of the lines imitates the rebounding of the voices of the victims:

> their moans
> The vales redoubled to the hills, and they
> To heaven.

Even the octave-sestet division is overridden by the continuous flow of the verse.

This must be the 'biggest' sonnet ever written. Its massiveness and perfect control are no doubt the result of Milton's long admiration for Virgil and the Italians. But they may also owe something to non-poetic influences. Milton had spent the past fifteen years writing essays and letters on a great variety of political and religious subjects, and the high, solemn style is something found much more frequently in seventeenth-century prose than in the verse of the period. Milton may have felt that in the writing of prose he had 'the use, as I may account it, but of my left hand' (*Reason of Church Government Urged*), but it is unlikely that his right hand did not know what his left hand was doing.

The great epic

When he came to write *Paradise Lost*, Milton did not discard all the poetic approaches he had been exploring in youth and middle age in order to replace them with something more suitable for epic poetry—the Grand Style. We have seen that his development was not only cumulative but accumulative: problems that puzzle him in one poem are resolved in another; the conflict between the Lady and Comus is worked out within the speaker of *Lycidas* and the sonnet to Lawrence uses the rose—Comus's emblem of the need to enjoy life while one can—along with the lily which is the Christian symbol of faith in the providence of God. *Paradise Lost* is on a larger scale than Milton's other works but its spaciousness means that he can allow himself still sharper contrasts than elsewhere, and still greater variety.

To start with, however, here is a famous and typical example of what everyone would agree is the Grand Style. It is part of our introduction to Satan, who, in an extremely rapid flashback, is first mentioned as the 'infernal serpent' and then as having been cast down from heaven for his pride.

St. Michael casting out the rebel angels, by Beccafumi (c. 1525)

40   He trusted to have equalled the most high,
              If he opposed; and with ambitious aim
              Against the throne and monarchy of God
              Raised impious war in heaven and battle proud
              With vain attempt. Him the almighty power
45   Hurled headlong flaming from the ethereal sky
              With hideous ruin and combustion down
              To bottomless perdition, there to dwell
              In adamantine chains and penal fire,
              Who durst defy the omnipotent to arms.

CRITICISM. The effect of this description is completely non-visual. We cannot imagine 'ethereal sky', 'hideous ruin', 'bottomless perdition', 'adamantine chains' or 'penal fire'; the adjectives, in fact, do not so much add to as cancel out any images we may already have (we are sure, for instance, that penal fire cannot look like ordinary fire, and this is confirmed later on when Milton tells us that these fires gave no light). Even the vision of Satan in flames conveys only a sense of something bright flashing past.

It is the sound of the passage that directs our response to it. The reader has to take a long breath as he embarks on lines 41 to 44; they obviously call for a crescendo, and so he lets his voice rise on the two long lines which insist first on the majesty of God and then on the outrageousness of Satan's assault on it. Expecting more of the same, he starts on line 44 and discovers that the great rebellion is over; anticlimax. Satan is then shoved aside, as it were, by the 'almighty power' which takes over the sentence and, with the tremendous force of 'hurled' at the beginning of the next line, sends him flying for four lines more until he lands in his bottomless pit.

The second part of the passage illustrates the kind of effect made possible by inversion and complex word order. In prose, lines 44–49 would probably go, 'The almighty power hurled him (who durst defy the omnipotent to arms) headlong flaming, etc.' Put like this, it would obviously lose the energy which its rhythm, and especially the position of 'hurled', now give it. More than that, it would cease to be an indirect statement of a view which is to be expressed more directly later on in Book I and enlarged on many times thereafter: that no action is possible outside the will and permission of God.

Although Satan is apparently described as an active character, he is constantly being transformed from a subject to an object. The transition from 'he' to 'him' reflects the moment at which he loses the power to act, and although the 'who' of the last line is the subject of 'durst', it is also grammatically related to 'him'. Milton keeps reminding us that Satan, despite his belief that he is acting under his own power, is really doing only what God permits him to do; it is only those characters who willingly do God's will who are free (hence Christ, and Milton himself as narrator, use the accusative 'me', while Satan is constantly saying 'I', and yet they are the active figures, not he). Only the original act of rebellion was his choice, which is why we are told, just before this quoted passage, that 'his pride', not God, 'Had cast him out from heaven'. When Raphael, in Book VI, comes to describe the actual moment of the fall of the angels, we find that they do not so much fall as jump; they could have turned back to Messiah, who pursues but does not run them down; it is because they can no longer bear the sight of him that

> headlong themselves they threw
> Down from the verge of heaven
> (VI. 864–5).

It is thus that Milton constantly underlines the paradox of a God whose service is perfect freedom and whose antagonist freely chooses to be, as Abdiel tells Satan, 'not free, but to thyself enthralled' (VI. 181).

Dr Johnson said that Milton's particular genius was for 'displaying the vast, illuminating the splendid, enforcing the awful, darkening the gloomy, and aggravating the dreadful'. The above passage certainly displays these qualities, especially the first of them. But there is more than this to Milton. He is also capable of evoking, as we have already seen in *L'Allegro*, an almost Dickensian atmosphere of innocent and wholehearted enjoyment. When Adam invites Raphael to stay for lunch with him and Eve, the ceremony of the scene and its built-in sermon on temperance do not destroy but rather enhance its charm.

Book V, 371–403

        Whom thus the angelic virtue answered mild.
        Adam, I therefore came, nor art thou such
        Created, or such place hast here to dwell,
        As may not oft invite, though spirits of heaven
375   To visit thee; lead on then where thy bower
        O'ershades; for these mid-hours, till evening rise
        I have at will. So to the silvan lodge
        They came, that like Pomona's arbour smiled
        With flowerets decked and fragrant smells; but Eve
380   Undecked, save with her self more lovely fair
        Than wood-nymph, or the fairest goddess feigned
        Of three that in Mount Ida naked strove,
        Stood to entertain her guest from heaven; no veil
        She needed, virtue-proof, no thought infirm
385   Altered her cheek. On whom the angel Hail
        Bestowed, the holy salutation used
        Long after to blest Marie, second Eve.

<pre>
                Hail mother of mankind, whose fruitful womb
                Shall fill the earth more numerous with thy sons
390   Than with these various fruits the trees of God
                Have heaped this table. Raised of grassy turf
                Their table was, and mossy seats had round,
                And on her ample square from side to side
                All autumn piled, though spring and autumn here
395   Danced hand in hand. A while discourse they hold;
                No fear lest dinner cool; when thus began
                Our author. Heavenly stranger, please to taste
                These bounties which our nourisher, from whom
                All perfect good unmeasured out, descends,
400   To us for food and for delight hath caused
                The earth to yield; unsavoury food perhaps
                To spiritual natures; only this I know,
                That one celestial Father gives to all
                                        (V. 371–403).
</pre>

EXPLANATORY NOTES. 'Virtue', in line 371, is the title of one of the orders of angels (as in the catalogue 'Thrones, dominations, princedoms, virtues, powers', which God uses and Satan frequently echoes in addressing his followers) and thus applied to Raphael, although he is in fact of higher rank. In lines 372–7 he assures Adam that *even* spirits of heaven will be glad to be invited by such a host; God has already given him permission to spend the rest of the day in Eden. Pomona (line 378) is a wood-nymph who, in Roman mythology, was responsible for gardens and fruit trees. The reference in lines 381–2 is to the story of the judgment of Paris, when Juno, Minerva and Venus came to Mount Ida and asked the young shepherd to decide which of them was the fairest; he gave the prize, an apple, to Venus because the goddess of love bribed him with a promise of the most beautiful woman in the world, Helen of Troy. Lines 385–7 are meant to foreshadow the Annunciation, when the angel Gabriel told Mary of the forthcoming birth of Christ in the words, 'Hail, thou that art highly favoured, the Lord is with thee: blessed art thou among women' (Luke 1:28). 'All autumn' in line 394 means all the fruits of autumn. Adam is 'our author'—that is, our ancestor; his speech is easier to follow if one adds a comma after 'good' in line 399. In its last lines, Adam is delicately enquiring whether what Raphael has just been offered is very different from what he is used to eating in heaven. Raphael's reply, which is an important statement of Milton's views about the relation of matter to spirit, is discussed on p. 52.

CRITICISM. The relations of Raphael, Adam and Eve are formal. When Adam goes to meet the angel (lines 350–7) Milton contrasts the simple dignity of his approach with the elaborate retinue of a prince on a state visit, but the impression left on our minds, as Milton intended, is that this *is* the meeting of two princes. Eve has stayed behind to prepare the lunch; she apparently never speaks to the angel at all, and even withdraws from their company some time after the meal (because, Milton says, she prefers to hear the whole conversation later on in Adam's own words). Raphael, however, greets her with great respect, and his title of 'mother of mankind' is to be echoed at several crucial points in the poem: Adam uses it when he is reconciled to her after the fall (XI. 158–61) and the last mention of her in the poem is as 'our mother Eve'.

Yet formality does not carry with it any idea of being uncomfortable. Eve does not blush on meeting Raphael (lines 384–5), and Adam is equally confident; he knows that the angel is a superior being, but since 'one celestial Father gives to all' he is not seriously afraid that what he has to offer will not be acceptable. Everything has always gone well in his world and Raphael is a messenger from an infinitely good and generous God. So there is a sense of gaiety in the image of spring and autumn dancing hand in hand—before the fall, Paradise enjoyed the best of all four seasons simultaneously —and in the famous 'No fear lest dinner cool' (because fire has not yet been invented), which suddenly brings before the mind, in comic contrast, *other* dinners and *other*, harassed, hostesses.

Milton's descriptions of Eden are written with a fallen world in mind, and they seldom fail to hint at the change to come. Even Raphael's gracious words to Adam, telling him that neither he nor his home is unworthy of an angelic guest, indirectly suggest the possibility of the very thing they deny. The square table on which Eve has piled her fruits and nuts is a symbol of temperance (because balanced and symmetrical) and thus a reminder of one of the causes of the fall. The whole idyllic scene will be recalled later on, when visitors from heaven seem a threat to the guilty couple instead of a cause for celebration.

Premonitions of the fall are most closely connected with Eve, who is surrounded here by an elaborate network of comparisions and allusions designed to suggest the ambivalence of her character. An allusion to Venus (goddess of love, but also causer of the Trojan war, and a 'feigned' character—Milton frequently qualifies his mythological references in this way) is balanced by an allusion to Mary, who was often paralleled with Eve in Biblical interpretations. We are probably meant to remember the importance of the apple in the judgment of Paris, and other references also associate Eve with fruits as part of a kind of sustained pun that runs through the poem: by eating the fruit, Eve will doom all the fruits of her womb to death, but one fruit of her action will be Christ's coming to save mankind and he also will be descended from her. The flower allusions also recur frequently in connection with Eve, suggesting both her frailty (she needs to be supported by her husband, her 'best prop'—IX. 433) and her beauty.

Moreover, by his insistence on Eve's purity and innocence, Milton keeps awakening the contrasting image of sensuality. As Alastair

An illustration from the 1688 edition of Paradise Lost *by Medina*

Fowler points out in his note on this passage, the expression 'virtue-proof' in line 384 can mean not only that Eve's virtue is her strength but also that she is proof against the 'angelic virtue', namely Raphael. Some forty lines after this, the possibility of angelic lust is again mentioned only to be rejected:

> Mean while at table Eve
> Ministered naked, and their flowing cups
> With pleasant liquors crowned: O innocence
> Deserving Paradise! If ever, then,
> Then had the sons of God excuse to have been
> Enamoured at that sight, but in those hearts
> Love unlibidinous reigned, nor jealousy
> Was understood, the injured lover's hell
> (443–50).

It may be rather tasteless of Milton to keep telling us what Raphael is *not* feeling, particularly when even to suggest the possibility of such feelings is to degrade the angel's character, but the effect is to remind us that a time is soon to come when Eve will be ashamed of her own nakedness, and when her love and Adam's will no longer be 'unlibidinous'. The fresh and charming pastoral scene must thus be interrupted occasionally by unexpected nightmare glimpses of a provocative Eve, a leering Raphael, and a jealous Adam. To return to Eden from these reminders of a post-lapsarian world is like coming out of the heat of the day into the cool bower in which the scene is set.

The speeches of Adam and Raphael in the above passage give only a faint idea of the variety of speaking voices in *Paradise Lost*. It is in the dialogues of Adam and Eve that the greatest range is found, reflecting the several stages of their development: formality of address ('daughter of God and man, accomplished Eve', IV. 660), the simplicity of Adam's lines quoted above, the heavy-handed compliments which accompany the fall—

> O glorious trial of exceeding love,
> Illustrious evidence, example high!
> (IX. 961–2.)

> Eve, now I see thou art exact of taste,
> And elegant, of sapience no small part
> (1017–18).

—the bickering that follows (see p. 74), and the humility of the last two books.

Among the supernatural characters, variety of tone is limited only by the impossibility of admitting any unpleasant emotions into the thoughts of the good angels. They cannot grieve for the misery which the fallen angels have brought on themselves or feel any doubts about their own righteousness. In such supremely rational beings, the actions of Satan can inspire only contempt or, at best, light irony. God is ironic even with the newly created Adam, but likeably so:

> A nice and subtle happiness I see
> Thou to thyself proposest, in the choice
> Of thy associates
>
> (VIII. 399–401),

is his reply to Adam's polite suggestion that he would rather not take a partner from among the animal kingdom. In other contexts, he can be more alarming, and his angels take their tone from him. We have already seen, in *Comus*, Milton's ability to express the lofty disdain felt by the righteous for those who are stupid enough to sin. In *Paradise Lost* most of the good angels take their turn at showing Satan up; most effective, perhaps, is Gabriel's succinct retort when his adversary calls him stupid:

> O loss of one in heaven to judge of wise,
> Since Satan fell, whom folly overthrew
>
> (IV. 904–5).

Satan, of course, is equally good at abuse: 'Not to know me argues your selves unknown', is his reply to two lesser angels who ask him to identify himself, though he is not allowed to have the last word in debate with the good characters. Devilish syntax is generally more complicated than that of God and the good angels; the father of lies deals in ambiguities and puns, and sometimes conceals the full implications of his words from himself as well as from others. The devils are fond of rhetoric as well: one of the reasons why their speeches are more dramatic than anyone else's is that they are also more public, because their loss of freedom forces them to play a part.

The formal oration was the basis of a gentleman's education in the Renaissance. Milton had read the speeches of Cicero in school, taken part in public debates at Cambridge, and probably heard an enormous amount of political rhetoric during the 1640s and 50s. No wonder the devils' speeches in the Pandemonium debate are so well done. Even F. R. Leavis, no unqualified admirer of *Paradise Lost*, admits that 'party politics in the Grand Style Milton can compass.' Moloch's ostentatious bluntness, Belial's slyness in pretending to agree with the previous speaker and then slipping in a completely new argument, Mammon's practical and complacent attitude, all have the air of being drawn from life. The following speech of Beelzebub comes at a point when most of his audience seem inclined to do what neither he nor Satan wants—resign themselves to defeat and make themselves at home in hell.

310   Thrones and imperial powers, offspring of heaven
        Ethereal virtues; or these titles now
        Must we renounce, and changing style be called
        Princess of hell? For so the popular vote
        Inclines, here to continue, and build up here
315   A growing empire; doubtless; while we dream,
        And know not that the king of heaven hath doomed
        This place our dungeon, not our safe retreat
        Beyond his potent arm, to live exempt
        From heaven's high jurisdiction, in new league
320   Banded against his throne, but to remain
        In strictest bondage, though thus far removed,
        Under the inevitable curb, reserved
        His captive multitude; for he, be sure
        In highth or depth, still first and last will reign
325   Sole king, and of his kingdom lose no part
        By our revolt, but over hell extend
        His empire, and with iron sceptre rule
        Us here, as with his golden those in heaven.
        What sit we then projecting peace and war?
330   War hath determined us, and foiled with loss
        Irreparable; terms of peace yet none
        Vouchsafed or sought; for what peace will be given
        To us enslaved, but custody severe,
        And stripes, and arbitrary punishment
335   Inflicted? And what peace can we return,
        But to our power hostility and hate,
        Untamed reluctance, and revenge though slow,
        Yet ever plotting how the conqueror least
        May reap his conquest, and may least rejoice
340   In doing what we most in suffering feel?
        Nor will occasion want, nor shall we need
        With dangerous expedition to invade
        Heaven, whose high walls fear no assault or siege,
        Or ambush from the deep. What if we find
345   Some easier enterprise?

EXPLANATORY NOTES. Beelzebub is simultaneously answering all three of the previous speakers. Mammon had recommended building up an empire in hell, hopefully suggesting that they might get acclimatized to its discomforts in time and find it not much inferior to heaven. To this Beelzebub points out that hell was designed as a place of punishment, not a separate kingdom; God will still be their ruler, as long as they remain in the place he intended for them. Belial had held out hope of God's relenting after a time and softening his treatment of them. Beelzebub denies this as well: there is thus no point in their remaining quiet in the hope of pardon. But in lines 341–4 he also rejects Moloch's desperate counsel of a second attack on heaven itself, which he sees as impossible. He will go on to unfold Satan's project for making a reconnaissance of the newly created world.

CRITICISM. Beelzebub's most effective rhetorical trick is copied from Satan's speech opening the meeting:

> Powers and dominions, deities of heaven,
> For since no deep within her gulf can hold
> Immortal vigour, though oppressed and fallen,
> I give not heaven for lost
>
> (II. 11–14).

By giving the fallen angels their old titles, Satan had proclaimed his confidence in their ability to regain them. By the time Beelzebub rises to speak, however, it is beginning to look as if the devils have lost interest in returning to heaven. So he uses the same terms in an even grander style:

> Thrones and imperial powers, offspring of heaven
> Ethereal virtues;

then, as the majestic names are still ringing in the air, he breaks off to ask whether, after all, they are prepared to settle for the rank of 'Princes of hell'.

The passage needs to be read aloud to get the full effect of this sudden turn, as something which seemed a mere formality, like 'Ladies and gentlemen', is discovered to be part of the speaker's argument. The irony becomes heavier as Beelzebub continues. He stresses the repeated 'here' in line 314 to remind them just what sort of place they are willing to establish their empire in, and then, after pretending to aquiesce in this rosy picture, he lets the full weight of his sarcasm fall on the single word 'doubtless'. Having now revealed his position, he changes his tone.

Beelzebub's strategy is to make the situation seem as desperate as possible, so that the solution he finally proposes will seem the only hope: Moloch and his kind can see it as heroic, and Belial and Mammon will recognize it as being, at any rate, 'easier' than the other alternatives. The stresses in this harsh speech fall on the harshest words, designed to wake the angels from their 'dream': 'doomed', 'dungeon', 'captive multitude', 'iron sceptre'. The sliding syntax makes it difficult to stop the argument at any point to examine it. For instance, in line 317, one is led to expect a pause after 'retreat', but instead the sense leads right on and one discovers that the 'not' of that line is being used not only to contrast 'dungeon' with 'retreat' but also for the larger contrast between 'to live exempt' and 'to remain in strictest bondage'. It would be possible to repunctuate in any of several ways, but the confusion is deliberate. Beelzebub is rushing on with his picture of the hard oppression to which the angels are doomed, and when he seems about to come to a full stop, as in line 323, a further thought carries him on again.

The question, 'What sit we here projecting peace and war?', is a rhetorical one because it is not intended to be answered. It is Beelzebub's way of saying that the preceding debate has been futile because they really have no choice. Despite the biting clarity of his manner, his words are full of double meanings. Milton originally spelled 'lose' in line 325 as 'loose'; a listener could hardly be expected to appreciate the pun, so it must have been intended for the reader, a small extra indication of Beelzebub's instinctive attraction to ambiguity. 'Determined' (line 330) means both 'ended, terminated', and 'decided'. The past participial constructions which follow— 'vouchsafed', 'enslaved', and 'inflicted'—can be taken either as verb forms or as adjectives. Since the word 'yet' in line 331 can mean either 'as of now' or 'nevertheless', the phrase

> terms of peace yet none
> Vouchsafed or sought

may be read either: 'Though we have been ruined by war, nevertheless no one has either offered or asked for peace', or 'So far, no peace terms have been either offered or sought'. While the difference in meaning, as opposed to the difference in grammar, is small, it helps to create a sense of vagueness as to who exactly might be likely to offer or seek for peace.

This vagueness fits with Beelzebub's policy, all through this speech, of talking as if everything had been the decision of all the angels instead of a private arrangement between the chairman and secretary of the meeting. 'What if we find Some easier enterprise?' has the air of a sudden inspiration on Beelzebub's part, but it is actually an idea which has been thrown out by Satan earlier on; if the other angels notice this, they have the sense not to say so. 'The want of human interest is always felt', Dr Johnson said of *Paradise Lost*, but in this little political drama the devils are all too human.

Another kind of human interest is provided by the 'digressions' in which Milton speaks in his own person. No other epic poet makes such use of the opportunities for personal intervention in his work, and Milton's early critics were somewhat uneasy about the lack of precedent for such frequent self-revelation, though they generally concluded, like Addison, that 'there is so great a beauty in these very digressions, that I would not wish them out of his poem'. In fact, the passages are not digressions at all, for Milton's relationship with his subject and his Muse is part of the story he has to tell. A poet who believes himself inspired by a Muse must regard himself not only as author but also as witness of the events of his poem. He must be able to descend to hell and ascend to heaven when the action requires it, and when, at the beginning of Book VII, it is time for him to return to earth, the downward movement is made to reflect both his state of mind and the emotional progression of the poem.

Book VII, 1–39

Descend from heaven Urania, by that name
If rightly thou art called, whose voice divine
Following, above the Olympian hill I soar,
Above the flight of Pegasean wing.
5   The meaning, not the name I call: for thou
Nor of the Muses nine, nor on the top
Of old Olympus dwell'st, but heavenly born,
Before the hills appeared, or fountain flowed,
Thou with eternal Wisdom didst converse,
10   Wisdom thy sister, and with her didst play
In presence of the almighty Father, pleased
With thy celestial song. Up led by thee
Into the heaven of heavens I have presumed,
An earthly guest, and drawn empyreal air,
15   Thy tempering; with like safety guided down
Return me to my native element:
Lest from this flying steed unreined, (as once
Bellerophon, though from a lower clime)
Dismounted, on the Aleian field I fall
20   Erroneous there to wander and forlorn.
Half yet remains unsung, but narrower bound
Within the visible diurnal sphere;
Standing on earth, not rapt above the pole,
More safe I sing with mortal voice, unchanged
25   To hoarse or mute, though fallen on evil days,
On evil days though fallen, and evil tongues;
In darkness, and with dangers compassed round,
And solitude; yet not alone, while thou
Visit'st my slumbers nightly, or when morn
30   Purples the east: still govern thou my song,
Urania, and fit audience find though few.
But drive far off the barbarous dissonance
Of Bacchus and his revellers, the race
Of that wild rout that tore the Thracian bard
35   In Rhodope, where woods and rocks had ears
To rapture, till the savage clamour drowned
Both harp and voice; nor could the Muse defend
Her son. So fail not thou, who thee implores:
For thou art heavenly, she an empty dream.

EXPLANATORY NOTES. Urania was the classical Muse of astronomy, but in calling 'the meaning, not the name', Milton is associating her with the Heavenly Muse first invoked by this name in a poem of Du Bartas (see the lines quoted on p. 84, which Milton seems to be echoing here). This Muse has been variously identified as the Logos (Second Person of the Trinity, by whom all things were made), as Divine Wisdom, and as the Holy Spirit; Milton seems to have thought of her as standing in the same relation to his poetic life as the Holy Spirit to his spiritual experience. Just as she differs from the Nine Muses of mythology in being real, not 'an empty dream', so the poet's spiritual journey has taken him higher than the classical heaven (situated on Mount Olympus), higher even than Pegasus, the winged horse, who was tamed and ridden by Bellerophon. But the story of Bellerophon had an unhappy ending, of which Milton also reminds himself: he finally had the audacity to fly to Olympus, and Jupiter punished him by allowing Pegasus to throw him; thus the hero ended his days wandering about the earth ('erroneous' in both senses of the word), blind and alone. As he begins the second half of his poem, Milton asks his Muse to protect him from Bellerophon's fate and from that of Orpheus, another symbol of poetic inspiration (see p. 151 for his story).

CRITICISM. 'Half yet remains unsung', though this is more obvious in the present form of *Paradise Lost* than it would have been in the first edition, which had only ten books. Symmetrical or not, this passage marks a turning point in the epic. Like Orpheus, Milton has descended into Hell and returned; like Bellerophon on his winged horse, he has mounted so high into the heavens that the Muse has had to 'temper' the rarefied atmosphere for his benefit. Now he is coming down to earth, and his story, for the most part, will stay there too, dealing henceforth with human, not divine, history. Perhaps for this reason, this third of Milton's four direct appeals to the Muse is the most sombre in tone. The openings of Books I and III suggested a pride in the vastness of the undertaking: Milton was about to tell 'Things unattempted yet in prose or rhyme' or 'things invisible to mortal sight'. But he is 'Standing on earth, not rapt above the pole', and that is why Urania is asked to descend from heaven.

All through the next books, Adam and Raphael echo this theme of descent. After hearing Raphael's account of the war in heaven— 'things above earthly thought'—Adam asks him to 'Deign to descend now lower' (VII. 84). Raphael gives him similar advice in answer to his astronomical questions:

> heaven is for thee too high
> To know what passes there; be lowly wise
> (VIII. 172–3).

and Adam at once agrees:

> Therefore from this high pitch let us descend
> A lower flight, and speak of things at hand
> (VIII. 198–9).

The final descent will occur when Adam comes down with Michael from the mountain of vision and then, hand in hand with Eve, continues his downward course from Paradise to 'the subjected plain' (XII. 640).

The style itself, after the fall, descends to a simpler level. It is significant that the next fine speech in the poem, Satan's gloating report on the success of his mission, is greeted by 'a dismal universal hiss' from his metamorphosed followers — Milton's way of debunking, once for all, the political oratory of his devils (X. 508). The repentance of Adam and Eve, on the other hand, is shown in the simplicity of their language. The last two books of *Paradise Lost* carry simplicity to the point almost of barrenness (foreshadowing the style of *Paradise Regained*) in such terse lines as Michael's

> Nor love thy life, nor hate; but what thou livest
> Live well, how long or short permit to heaven
>
> (XI. 553–4).

But Adam's final summing up of what he has learned—

> that to obey is best,
> And love with fear the only God, to walk
> As in his presence, ever to observe   .
> His providence, and on him sole depend,
> Merciful over all his works, with good
> Still overcoming evil, and by small
> Accomplishing great things
>
> (XII. 561–7)

—shows how moving this simplicity can be when it comes after so many self-torturing thoughts and confused aspirations.

If Milton as spectator watches the gradual descent of Adam and Eve from vain ambition to humble resignation, Milton as author is also showing that he himself has learned the same lesson. The recognition is important, because the audacity of Bellerophon is a close analogue not only to Satan's rebellion, the subject of the previous book, but also to Milton's own 'adventurous song' (I. 13), which has perhaps 'presumed' in daring to tell of things so far above mortal knowledge. This is why, despite Bacchus and his revellers and the other dangers of Restoration England, despite his awareness of being only a 'mortal voice' and a writer whose audience will be small, he can describe himself as 'more safe' now that he has returned to earth.

6 Some myths

The Renaissance humanists knew that there were Greek and Roman myths about a great flood, a hero whose strength lay in his hair, a miraculous birth and a hero who died and was restored to life. This did not make them think that Christianity was a fairy tale; rather, it seemed to them to prove that there was one true religion of which all human beings had been granted some shadowy glimpses. The immense popularity of the classical legends in medieval and Renaissance literature can be explained by two factors: first, they could be treated with a great deal more freedom than a seriously held religion; second, they lent themselves to allegorical interpretation. The extreme humanist position, however, came close to saying that all religions were of equal value, and in some Renaissance works paganism and Christianity seem almost interchangeable.

Though Milton, throughout his life, was attracted by the Platonic doctrine that everything on earth was only a copy of an ideal original which existed in another world, he did not place his own religion on the same level as all the others. Christianity, for him, was literally true, while the classical myths were either symbols of it or allegories of moral truths. In his later works he is at pains to use comparisons of biblical and classical themes only to show the inferiority of the latter. But no one who had been soaked in the *Aeneid* and Ovid's *Metamorphoses* from childhood on could altogether discard stories which he knew as well as those of the Bible. There is no doubt that the classical myths meant a great deal to Milton, not so much for their inherent charm as for the other meanings which had been read into them for generations. The following are a few of the ones with which he seems to have identified himself most closely.

Circe

The original Circe appears in Homer's *Odyssey* as a rather capricious goddess who could, however, be a useful friend if one knew how to manage her. Odysseus and his men land on her island and she transforms some of them into swine, with the aid of a magic potion. The god Hermes (or Mercury) appears to Odysseus and tells him how to defeat her charms by means of a magic herb. The hero follows this advice, gets Circe into his power, becomes her lover, and makes her free his men, though apparently he does nothing about the other victims on the island. A year of feasting follows, and even when the Greeks have decided to resume their journey Circe remains on friendly terms with them and gives them good advice.

It was the first part of this story that allegorists found most useful. Because the magician was a woman and because she wrought her spells by a magic drink, it was easy to see her as a symbol of the power of lust and drunkenness to reduce men to the level of beasts. Most of the *femme fatale* figures of Renaissance epic are imitated from Circe, and the ending of Spenser's second book of *The Faerie Queene*, which deals with temperance, is an almost complete allegorization of the *Odyssey*.

The resemblance of the Circe story to that of *Comus* is obvious, but it had been a popular subject for many earlier masques, since the beast-men provided good parts for antimasquers (see p. 96). Because the central character was to be a young girl, Milton's tempter had to be the son of Circe rather than Circe herself. But the enchanted cup and the counter-magic provided by a messenger from heaven are very close to Homer.

The Attendant Spirit of *Comus* seems to stand halfway between the pagan Mercury and the angel Raphael, who is compared to Mercury when he first lights on earth in *Paradise Lost* (V. 285–7). This resemblance is not just a coincidence, for Raphael, among his other duties, has to warn Adam against the magic power which Eve exerts over him by 'the charm of beauty's powerful glance' (VIII. 533). Eve is more explicitly compared to Circe later on when, just before the fall, she is described as being able to summon all the beasts,

> more duteous at her call,
> Than at Circean call the herd disguised
> (IX. 521–2).

After she has succumbed to the temptation of the serpent, she plays the role of Circe in earnest by offering Adam the fruit that will transform him into a beast, while Satan, who thinks himself safe in hell, suddenly finds himself undergoing an animal metamorphosis which symbolizes his own spiritual degeneration.

Orpheus

The story of Orpheus was as obvious a subject for opera as that of Circe for masque, since it was about a musician and the effect of his songs. His legend is even more widespread than Circe's and was the object of a special religious cult.

Orpheus was the son of Calliope, the Muse of epic poetry. He had a lyre that was given him by Apollo and when he played and sang the trees and stones moved out of their places to hear him. He was able to calm men's quarrels too, but his greatest achievement was his persuading Pluto to free his wife Eurydice from the underworld—the episode which forms the subject of Monteverdi's opera (see p. 18) and many others. The fact that this story ended unhappily, with Orpheus losing Eurydice again, gave trouble to many composers. The first operatic version, by Peri, disregarded tradition and supplied an ending which reunited the couple, but Monteverdi's librettist, Striggio, was more honest. So honest, in fact, that he originally intended the opera to end with the death of its hero; Monteverdi substituted the ascent into heaven which transformed the story into an allegory of the power of music. What actually happened to Orpheus, according to the legend, was much less beautiful: he was torn limb from limb by women, followers of the god Dionysus (or Bacchus).

In the classical tradition, from very early on, Orpheus was a symbol of the divinely inspired artist. Christian allegorists made him one of the many pagan prototypes of Christ, because of his descent into hell and safe return (even the fact that Eurydice had been killed by a serpent's sting made her a fitting parallel to Christ's 'bride', the Christian Church). Orpheus's failure to keep his word about not looking back on Eurydice could be taken, as we have seen it was in Monteverdi's opera, to show that even the greatest men are unable to withstand the power of passion. Finally, the manner of his death was both ironic (the artist can save others but not himself) and a bitter comment on the inferiority of irrational man to the trees and stones of the natural world.

The Orpheus story is, in fact, a reversal of Circe's, in that one tells how lust can reduce man to the level of beasts while the other is about the power of art to lift him to divinity. Both the Lady in *Comus* and the Attendant Spirit have Orpheus's ability to enchant those who hear them sing. The Spirit in his shepherd's disguise

> Well knows to still the wild winds when they roar,
> And hush the waving woods
>
> (85–7).

And the Lady's song, which the Spirit thinks capable of bringing the dead to life again, fills Comus with wonder. He has heard enchanted songs before, from his mother Circe and the Sirens—who, in the *Odyssey*, lure those sailors who hear them to their death on the rocks—but he recognizes a difference:

> they in pleasing slumber laid the sense,
> And in sweet madness robbed it of itself
>
> (255–60),

whereas the Lady makes him feel not madness but a 'sober certainty of waking bliss' (261). There are, then, two kinds of music (the devils in *Paradise Lost* can sing too). In *An Apology for Smectymnuus* Milton seems to suggest that there are also two kinds of Circe, the evil enchantress and the goddess 'whose charming cup is only virtue which she bears in her hand to those who are worthy'. Orpheus and Circe thus turn out to be ambiguous figures on the Platonic ladder, neither good nor evil in themselves, but only in the use they make of their powers.

The tragic ending of Orpheus, which Milton uses unforgettably in *Lycidas* (58–63), seems to have had a more personal meaning for him than any other myth. All his life he tended to see himself as one cut off from his fellow men, surrounded by hostile and insensitive barbarians. He hinted as much to an audience of Cambridge students in one of his Prolusions; in *Sonnet XII* he tells how, on the publication of his divorce tracts,

> straight a barbarous noise environs me
> Of owls and cuckoos, asses, apes and dogs.

Circe's beasts and Bacchus's 'rout that made the hideous roar' (*Lycidas*, 61) are alike in their barbarity. Milton was probably thinking of Orpheus when he wrote, in his last political tract before the Restoration, 'Thus much I should perhaps have said though I were sure I should have spoken only to trees and stones'. If so, he must also have remembered that, although 'woods and rocks had ears' to the songs of Orphèus (*PL* VII. 35), his Dionysiac murderers had drowned the music with their own cries. In the invocation to Urania which has already been discussed (pp. 145–47), we have seen that Milton ends by reminding himself that Orpheus's protectress, .the Muse Calliope, was fictitious and the Christian poet must rely on heaven alone. But it is only the Muse who is dismissed as an 'empty dream'; Bacchus and his revellers remain frighteningly real.

Hercules

Hercules is, among other things, a pagan counterpart of Samson, who resembles him in his strength and his susceptibility to women. The son of Zeus and a mortal woman, he strangled serpents while still a baby (*Nativity Ode*, 227–8), and as a man performed an enormous number of feats of strength, including the famous 'twelve labours' imposed on him by the King of the House of Perseus. His legend is complicated by the inclusion of so many different local traditions (the Greeks were always glad to adopt the gods and heroes of other cultures), but from the viewpoint of the Christian allegorists the most interesting would have been those which paralleled biblical episodes: the three days which he spent in the belly of a monster (like Jonah); his descent into the underworld, which makes him another prototype of Christ, and his restoring of the dead Alcestis to her husband (see *Sonnet XIX*); his ascent into heaven after his death. Milton's *The Passion* compares Christ to him:

> Most perfect hero, tried in heaviest plight
> Of labours huge and hard, too hard for human wight
> (13–14).

His sonnet to Fairfax pictures the general as performing one of the labours of Hercules in cutting off the Hydra's heads of rebellion.

Proserpina

Proserpina was the daughter of Ceres, goddess of growing crops. She was carried off by Pluto, god of the underworld, and obliged to spend three months of the year with him because while in his domain she had swallowed a few pomegranate seeds. During her absence Ceres mourns, crops do not grow, and this is why there is such a season as winter. In *Paradise Lost*, Milton several times identifies Eve with Proserpina and Satan with Pluto (e.g. IV. 268–72; IX. 395–6; and the various references to Satan as 'the grisly king', 'the prince of darkness', etc.). Because of its effect on the eternal spring of the earth, the rape of Proserpina is an appropriate symbol of the fall of man.

Gardens

The Garden of Eden has many classical parallels. One is the description of the Golden Age, or reign of Saturn, as found in, e.g. the first book of the *Metamorphoses*. It was often imitated by early Christian writers on the Creation. Other happy gardens were the Elysian Fields of the classical underworld and the Garden of the Hesperides, sacred to Juno, where a serpent was twined round a tree of golden apples to protect them from theft (but Hercules did steal some in the course of one of his Labours). The Garden of Adonis, to which the Attendant Spirit is bound at the end of *Comus*, is a Spenserian invention, based on the legend of the boy who was loved by both Venus and Proserpina and therefore required, after his death, to spend half the year on earth and half in the underworld. Spenser imagined a garden in which all life originated and where Adonis enjoyed eternal youth and love with Venus; Milton's reinterpretation of the allegory makes Adonis lie there recovering slowly from the wound which killed him.

Wars in heaven

The Greeks thought of Olympian history as a series of rebellions by sons against their father. First Uranus cast the Cyclopes (one-eyed giants) out of heaven into Tartarus; then his other sons the Titans dethroned him; they in turn were dethroned by the Olympian gods in alliance with the Cyclopes. There were other, unsuccessful revolts against the Olympians by the giants and by the snakey monster Typhon (see *Nativity Ode*, 226). Milton remembered many details of these accounts, such as the nine days which it took the Cyclopes to fall from heaven to Tartarus (cf. *PL* VI. 871) and the use of divine thunder against the uprooted rocks of the rebels, in his description of the war in heaven. The story of Prometheus, a Titan who sided with Zeus in his war on the Titans and was then punished with eternal tortures for giving the gift of fire to mankind when Zeus wanted to destroy him, is sometimes compared with Satan's, but the two cases are really very different; Satan wants to destroy man, Prometheus, like Christ, suffers for him. But the heroic defiance of the hero in Aeschylus's *Prometheus Bound*, like its descriptions of cosmic struggle, may well be reflected in *Paradise Lost*.

Further reading

A useful, well-illustrated introduction to the subject is M. GRANT, *Myths of the Greeks and Romans* (Weidenfeld & Nicolson, 1962). D. BUSH, *Mythology and the Renaissance Tradition in English Poetry* (Pageant, 1957) looks at sixteenth- and seventeenth-century treatments of myth and includes a chapter on Milton. The existence of so many different versions of the same stories in widely separated cultures has naturally led modern scholars, like those of the Renaissance, to look for the common experience lying behind them. Everyone knows Freud's term 'the Oedipus complex'; this is typical of the way in which modern psychologists have interpreted the myths as allegories of human sexual experience. On the other hand, ROBERT GRAVES, whose *The Greek Myths* (2 vols, Penguin, 1955, 1960) is a fascinating and thorough summary of the legends and their variants, thinks that they reflect the change from a matriarchal to a patriarchal structure in society and religion, and should be studied as anthropology rather than psychology. Anyone interested in following up this line of approach ought to compare the Greek myths with those of other cultures; good places to start are the Larousse *Encyclopedia of Mythology* and *Myth, Sacred History, and Philosophy*, by CORNELIUS LOEW (Harcourt, Brace & World, 1967).

Short biographies

BACON, FRANCIS, 1561–1626. Politician, essayist, philosopher, scientist. Had a highly successful government career, rising to become Lord Chancellor and Baron Verulam in 1618, but lost his place and was disgraced in 1621 for taking bribes. Author of *Essays* (1597, extensively added to in 1612 and 1625), *Advancement of Learning* (1605), and numerous English and Latin proposals for a reform of education and development of experimental science. Royal Society (chartered 1661) looked back to him as their true founder.

BUCKINGHAM, GEORGE VILLIERS, 1ST DUKE OF, 1592–1628. Favourite of James I and later Charles I, whose assassination by a Puritan fanatic was greeted by great popular rejoicing. As an influence on the foreign and domestic policy of both kings, he was disastrous, but Charles I may have learned something from his enthusiasm for art.

BUNYAN, JOHN, 1628–88. Preacher and writer, by trade a tinker, soldier on Parliamentary side during Civil War, later itinerant preacher. Imprisoned in 1660, and wrote many of his works in jail. These include *Grace Abounding* (1666), *Pilgrim's Progress* (Part I, 1678, Part II, 1684) and *The Life and Death of Mr Badman* (1680).

COMENIUS, JOHN AMOS, 1592–1670. Educational reformer, Moravian by birth, wanted to see state-supported schools in every town, for all boys and girls of normal intelligence. Paid a visit to England in 1641, encouraged by M.'s friend Hartlib, but nothing came of it, despite some Parliamentary interest in his schemes. His educational principles differed from M.'s not only in being more democratic but also in stressing practical and technical rather than literary studies.

COPERNICUS, NICHOLAS, 1473–1543. Polish-born; studied at Cracow, Bologna, Padua. Early training was theological and legal but he had wide interests including astronomy. In 1510 his reading of Pythagoras and other ancient writers (he made very few observations of the sky himself) led him to devise a new mathematical explanation of the universe, still based on the circle, but assuming that the sun rather than the earth was the centre of the system. His hypothesis was not published until the year of his death, and, before 1600, was not maintained to be literally true but only one of several possible alternatives to the geocentric view.

CROMWELL, OLIVER, 1599–1658. Cambridge-educated, member of Long Parliament. After seeing service at Battle of Edgehill, returned to his native East Anglia to build up Eastern Association Army: it was largely responsible for victory of Marston Moor, 1644, and became nucleus of cavalry in New Model Army, formed the following year. Sought execution of Charles I only after concluding that negotiation with him was hopeless. Though a believer in religious toleration and sympathetic towards Levellers, had to compromise on both points after attaining power. Lord Protector, 1653–58.

DATI, CARLO, 1619–76. Florentine scholar and writer, secretary of

Academy della Crusca and later professor of Latin and Greek at Florentine Academy. Met M. on his Italian Journey and exchanged letters with him in 1640s.

DIODATI, CHARLES (?1609–38). Born of Italian father, English mother, with many relatives on the Continent; M. visited his family home in Lucca. Probably met M. at St Paul's school. Surviving letters suggest he was of a lively and cheerful temperament. After taking Oxford degrees, studied theology for a year in Geneva, then apparently gave it up and returned to England to study and practise medicine.

DONNE, JOHN, 1572–1631. Brought up as a Catholic and did not leave the Church until his twenties. Originally intended career at court, but lost his place and suffered many years of poverty because of secret marriage to employer's niece. Ordained 1615. Dean of St Paul's, 1621–31. Author of witty and passionate love poems, satires, religious verse; also an eloquent preacher. Only poems to be published in his lifetime were the two *Anniversaries* (1611 and 1612).

DRYDEN, JOHN, 1631–1700. Came from Puritan background and wrote verses on death of Cromwell but after Restoration became a court writer of plays, satires (*Absalom and Achitophel*, 1681–2), translations, and many poems and critical essays. Lost his post as Poet Laureate, 1688, because he had become a Catholic during James II's reign. Was the first critic of *Paradise Lost* to say that Satan, technically speaking, is poem's hero.

ELLWOOD, THOMAS, 1639–1713. Became a Quaker in 1660 and spent much of his life in prison for his beliefs. Author of many Quaker tracts and editor of journals of George Fox, leader of the movement. Read aloud to M. in 1663 and was taught Latin by him; wrote elegy on M.'s death.

FAIRFAX, THOMAS, 1612–71. After outstanding military successes in early years of Civil War, became Commander in Chief of New Model Army, 1645. Refused to take part in trial and sentencing of Charles I but continued to serve Commonwealth until 1650, when he resigned his commission rather than make war on Scots, which he felt would be breach of 1643 Covenant. Retired to his estate at Nun Appleton, devoted himself to literature and collection of antiquities, later was instrumental in bringing about Restoration.

GALILEI, GALILEO, 1564–1642. Like M., the son of an amateur musician. Using telescope, invented in Netherlands, he was first astronomer to confirm Copernican hypothesis by observation. His *Siderius Nuncius*, or *Starry Messenger* (1610) revealed existence of four moons of Jupiter, mountains of the Moon, and true nature of Milky Way. In 1613 he described spots on the sun; 1616, Holy Office extracted his promise to publish no more astronomical works but in 1632 he broke this agreement and was forced to make recantation

THREE REPUBLICAN LEADERS
Cromwell, our chief of men
Fairfax, whose name in arms through Europe rings
Vane, young in years, but in sage council old

of his views, ending life as a prisoner at his villa in Arcetri, near Florence.

GILL, ALEXANDER, the younger, ?1597–1644. Teacher and friend of M. at St Paul's School, where he succeeded his father, also Alexander Gill, as headmaster in 1635.

HALL, JOSEPH, 1574–1656. Before entering Church in 1601, well-known as author of, e.g. *Toothless Satires* (1597), which he thought (wrongly) were first verse satires in English. Rose to become Bishop of Norwich, though his tolerance of Puritanism made Laud suspect him of leanings toward it. His pro-Episcopal pamphlets express a moderate's reaction to extreme reformers. Imprisoned with the other bishops in December 1641, then freed on bail with his estate forfeited; despite persecution, was loyal to Church until his death.

HARTLIB, SAMUEL, ?1596–?1662. Prussian-born, settled in England in 1628. Indefatigable writer of pamphlets on, e.g., educational reform, international union of all Protestants, and improved husbandry. Friend of M., who wrote *Of Education* at his request.

HERBERT, GEORGE, 1593–1633. Public Orator at Cambridge in M.'s time. Son of a distinguished family, originally intended career at court but renounced this to enter Church in 1625. Became rector at Bemerton, near Salisbury, in 1630 and apparently led a life of exemplary dedication. Most poems in *The Temple* (published after his death) probably date from this period or not long before.

JONES, INIGO, ?1572–1652. Scene-designer and architect. On visits to Italy he learned how to create elaborate scenic effects at court masques and also acquired a great admiration for Palladian architecture which he introduced into England. Built Banqueting House at Whitehall (1619–22), the Queen's House at Greenwich (1617–35), and many other buildings now destroyed or excessively restored. Royalist and Roman Catholic.

JONSON, BEN, 1572–1637. Bricklayer, soldier and actor in his youth, became a great scholar with honorary degrees from both Oxford and Cambridge. The most respected, if not loved, dramatist of the century; plays include *Volpone* (1607), *The Alchemist* (1612), *Bartholomew Fair* (1614). Began writing court masques in collaboration with Inigo Jones in 1605, later quarrelled with him and satirized him in verse and on the stage. The first English poet laureate.

KEPLER, JOHANNES, 1571–1630. One of the earliest supporters of Copernican hypothesis. Wrote work on optics, devised improved lens for telescope, and explained principles of planetary motion in elliptical orbits (still known as Kepler's Laws) in *Astronomia Nova* (1609) and *De Harmonice Mundi* (1619).

KING, EDWARD, 1612–37. Born in Ireland, entered Christ's College,

Cambridge, 1626; elected, by special royal mandate, to a fellowship there in 1630. Author of some Latin poems. Drowned on his way to Ireland to visit his family. Amid general panic as the ship went down, he is said to have knelt on the deck and prayed.

LAUD, WILLIAM, 1573–1645. After a career marked by obstinacy, incorruptibility, and hostility to nonconformity in religion, he became Archbishop of Canterbury in 1633. His influence in secular as well as spiritual matters was much resented and in 1641 he was arrested by Parliament. His private papers, seized in 1643, were used against him at his trial, which was a frank act of vindictiveness on the part of the more extreme Puritans; in 1645, he was executed.

LAWES, HENRY, 1596–1662. With his brother William, among the most distinguished of Caroline musicians. M. may have met him through his father. He set to music M.'s songs in *Arcades* and *Comus*, also the short lyric *On a May Morning*. Music teacher of Egerton family, Gentleman of the Chapel Royal, member of King's private music. M. is one of several poets who praise him for his skill at setting words to music.

LAWRENCE, EDWARD, ?1633–57. Son of Henry Lawrence (1600–64), a Puritan statesman and President of the Council of State under the Commonwealth. Edward was a friend and possibly a pupil of M.'s. He became an M.P. the year before his early death.

LILBURNE, JOHN, 1615–57. First imprisoned at twenty-one for importing forbidden books from Holland. Released through Cromwell's intercession in 1641, fought in Civil War and rose to become Lieutenant-Colonel. Imprisoned again, this time by Parliament for printing unlicensed books and refusing to take Covenant, he made study of English law, especially Magna Charta, and developed Leveller principles which he proclaimed in many underground pamphlets. After collapse of Leveller movement, was tried for treason to Commonwealth, but acquitted amid cheers of the people. 'Freeborn John' died a prisoner, having returned illegally to England after being exiled in 1652. Became a Quaker in his last years.

MANSO, GIOVANNI BATTISTA, *c.* 1560–1645. Marquis of Villa, devoted his fortune to patronage of art and literature. Poet, also founder of Academy of Oziosi, who met in his palace. Friend and biographer of Tasso, who named his *Dialogue on Friendship* after him. M. was well-treated by him on his visit to Naples and wrote him a poem expressing his gratitude.

MARVELL, ANDREW, 1621–78. Royalist and Anglican in background. In 1651 became tutor to Fairfax's daughter at Nun Appleton. M. recommended him for government service in 1653 but he did not get the post of assistant to M. until 1657, acting in the meantime as tutor to a ward of Cromwell's. Elected M.P. for Hull in 1659, and continued to represent it until his death. Most of his poetry, except for political satires, apparently dates from early 1650s. It was first published after his death.

PHILLIPS, EDWARD, 1630–?96, and JOHN, 1631–1706. M.'s nephews, who lived with him during their adolescence and were educated by him, both ended up with political convictions very different from his. Edward was the more serious: his works include a dictionary, a history, survey of poets of all ages, with critical comments, and the translation of M.'s *Letters of State* to which he prefaced a memoir of M. But like his brother, he was also a hack writer of poems, novels and comic works. John seems to have reacted against his Puritan background in *Satire Against Hypocrites* (1655); he acted as propagandist for Titus Oates during Popish Plot scare (1678–82), translated *Don Quixote* (1687) and ran a successful political and literary periodical.

PRYNNE, WILLIAM, 1600–69. Author of over two hundred books and pamphlets (attacks on long hair, drinking healths, stage plays, religious nonconformity, etc.). Twice pilloried and had his ears sawn off, once for *Histriomastix* (1633) which attacked plays at a time when Henrietta Maria had just acted in a private court performance, and once for writing against Laud. Released from prison (1641) by Long Parliament, of which he soon became one of most bigoted members; expelled and imprisoned by Cromwell, later supported the Restoration and was rewarded by Charles II.

SAUMAISE, CLAUDE, 1588–1658. French-born, a convert to Protestantism, internationally-known scholar who taught himself Hebrew, Arabic, Coptic and other Eastern languages, and wrote more than fifty works. Professor at University of Leyden and guest at court of Queen Christiana of Sweden; now remembered only as M.'s antagonist.

SMECTYMNUUS. Pseudonym of five Presbyterian ministers, Stephen Marshall (1594–1655), Edmund Calamy (1600–66), Thomas Young (1587–1666), Matthew Newcomen (1610–66) and William Spurstowe (1605–67). Basically moderate, they opposed execution of Charles I and refused to take 1650 oath to support Commonwealth. Thomas Young, M.'s former tutor, was group's leader in early 1640s; in 1644 he became Master of Jesus College, Cambridge. M. probably broke with Smectymnuuns in that year or earlier, due to the generally hostile Presbyterian reception of his divorce pamphlets.

SPENSER, EDMUND, 1552–99. Most famous poet of his time, but spent his life in unsuccessful search for advancement at court, despite patronage of Sidney, Leicester and Ralegh. After publication of *Shepherd's Calendar* (1579), went to Ireland as secretary to Queen's deputy, Lord Grey, in 1580 and was later granted an estate there, where he wrote *Faerie Queene* (first three books, 1590, IV–VI, 1596); his castle was burnt in Irish rebellion of 1598, and he died in London the following year. His funeral, paid for by Essex, was attended by most poets of the time, who cast their elegies into his grave.

TASSO, TORQUATO, 1544–95. Italian poet who wrote his first epic at seventeen, thus winning his father's permission to turn from law to study of literature and philosophy. Shortly after publication of his *Jerusalem Delivered* (1575), began to show signs of insanity and was confined to a hospital from 1579 to 1586. Spent his last years wandering restlessly around Italy and stayed for a time with Manso in Naples. Died in Rome; onset of his last illness prevented him from receiving laurel crown intended for him by the Pope.

VANE, HENRY, the younger, 1613–62. Became Puritan at fifteen, went to New England in 1635 and was elected governor of Massachusetts Bay Colony; returned to England, 1637, after losing election over issue of religious tolerance, of which he was always an advocate. An M.P. and friend of Cromwell, took no part in King's trial but became efficient member of Council of State until Cromwell's dissolution of Parliament in 1653, when he retired to spend his time in religious speculation. His unorthodox and mystical views made him suspect both to Commonwealth leaders, who imprisoned him briefly in 1656, and to the Restored monarchy which executed him after a trial in which he showed great courage.

WINSTANLEY, GERRARD. Nothing is known of this unlearned but eloquent writer except during the period (1649–52) when he organized Digger movement for communal cultivation of land and addressed appeals for an egalitarian society to City of London, Army, and Cromwell. Generally ridiculed and ignored; even the Leveller, Lilburne, thought it too much a minority movement to be valid.

WOTTON, HENRY, 1568–1639. One of the best minor poets of his time, also diplomat, linguist, art collector, friend of Donne and Isaac Walton. Three times ambassador to Venice; wrote M. a friendly letter in 1637, praising *Comus* and advising him how to behave in Italy.

YOUNG, THOMAS, *see* SMECTYMNUUS.

Bibliography

Lives of Milton

The most complete and scholarly modern biography is by W. R. PARKER (2 vols, Oxford U.P., 1968). A shorter life that is quite readable is *John Milton, Englishman,* by J. H. HANFORD (Gollancz, 1950).

Scientific background

C. S. LEWIS, *The Discarded Image* (Cambridge U.P., 1964) is an entertaining account of the intellectual background to medieval and renaissance literature. More detailed information about the macrocosm can be found in A. J. MEADOWS, *The High Firmament* (Leicester U.P., 1969), a study of astronomy in literature, and M. H. NICOLSON, *The Breaking of the Circle* (Columbia U.P., 1960), which gives many examples of how the 'new science' affected the poetry of Milton and his contemporaries. On the microcosm, see J. B. BAMBOROUGH, *The Little World of Man* (Longmans, 1952), a study of renaissance psychology and physiology. A great deal of useful information is also assembled in the annotated *Poems of John Milton* (ed. J. CAREY and A. FOWLER, Longmans, 1968), particularly in the introduction to *Paradise Lost,* which is available separately in paperback.

Political and religious background

Classic studies of Puritanism and the Civil War are W. HALLER, *The Rise of Puritanism* (Columbia U.P., 1938) and D. M. WOLFE, *Milton in the Puritan Revolution* (Nelson, 1941). A short, clear, though somewhat controversial history of the period is C. HILL, *The Century of Revolution* (Nelson, 1961), while G. M. TREVELYAN, *England under the Stuarts* (Methuen, 1904; Pelican, 1960) gives an old-fashioned, unashamedly emotional account of the same period. Both these historians are pro-Puritan; it might be well to compare them with C. V. WEDGWOOD's well-written and Royalist-biased *The King's Peace* and *The King's War* (Collins, 1955, 1958, and Fontana, 1966).

Many of the works on Milton's religion make difficult reading, but B. RAJAN, *Paradise Lost and the Seventeenth Century Reader* (Chatto, 1947) provides a useful corrective to some of the more complicated theories that have been built on a reading of Milton's prose, by considering how far the author's private views can actually be found in his poetry. C. S. LEWIS, *Preface to Paradise Lost* (Oxford U.P., 1942, Oxford paperbacks, 1960) includes a chapter summarizing Milton's debt to Augustine.

Literary background

The standard work on Milton's literary period is D. BUSH, *English Literature in the Earlier Seventeenth Century* (Oxford U.P., 1945). The *Donne to Marvell* volume in the popular Pelican Guide to English Literature (ed. BORIS FORD, 1956) gives very little space to Milton but is a reasonably comprehensive survey of his times. More detailed studies of Milton's relation to specific literary kinds include J. G. DEMARAY, *Milton and the Masque Tradition* (Harvard U.P., 1968), F. T. PRINCE, *The Italian Element in Milton's Verse* (Oxford U.P., 1954), C. M. BOWRA, *From Virgil to Milton* (Macmillan, 1945, Papermac, 1965), the essays collected in *Milton's Lycidas, the Tradition and the Poem* (ed. C. A. PATRIDES, Holt, 1961), and W. R. PARKER, *Milton's Debt to Greek Tragedy in Samson Agonistes* (Johns Hopkins U.P., 1937).

Imitators and critics

The serious eighteenth- and nineteenth-century imitations of *Paradise Lost* are among the dullest works in the English language; the only exception is KEATS's *Hyperion*, which the young poet nevertheless abandoned in despair when he felt that it was becoming too Miltonic. TENNYSON, though he praised the 'God-gifted organ voice' of Milton, preferred his more lush descriptive passages in *Comus* and the scenes in the Garden of Eden (see his *Milton* and, for a Tennysonian description of Eden, *The Lotus-Eaters*) to the grand epic effects.

In comic and satiric poetry, however, the grand style very soon found its home. DRYDEN, in *Absalom and Achitophel* (1681), was the first to discover how it could be used to elevate realistic and topical subjects while at the same time bringing out the ridiculous contrast between the true nature of his characters and the epic heroes for whom he pretended to take them. Obvious Miltonic phrases, such as 'Him staggering so when hell's dire agent found', are rare in Dryden; the first stylistic parody of *Paradise Lost*, which is still the best one, was *The Splendid Shilling* (1705), done as a labour of love by JOHN PHILLIPS (no relation to Milton's nephews). But the greatest practitioners of the mock-heroic style were POPE and BYRON. Pope's *Rape of the Lock* (1714) and *The Dunciad* (1729) are full of epic echoes: the sylphs and gnomes of *The Rape* carry on a version of the War in Heaven and the second book of *The Dunciad* begins with a deliberate reminiscence of the second book of *Paradise Lost*. Byron, who had been accused of belonging to a 'Satanic School' of poetry, responded like many Romantics by identifying himself with Satan the rebel; his *Vision of Judgement* (1822) succeeds admirably in reconciling the real impressiveness of its Byronic-Miltonic Satan with the satiric spirit of its attack on tyranny and sycophancy. The figure of the 'archangel ruined', whether in human form or divine, dominates literature of the early nineteenth century; see the chapter on 'The Metamorphoses of Satan' in MARIO PRAZ, *The Romantic Agony* (Oxford U.P., 1933; Fontana 1960). Perhaps the nearest thing to a modern *Paradise Lost* is J. R. R. TOLKIEN's *The Lord of the Rings* (Allen & Unwin, 1954–55, paperback 1968). One notices, however, that the arch-villain, Sauron, is carefully kept from becoming the central figure of the book; he is a background threat rather than a character in whom one can take interest. It seems likely that Tolkien chose this technique of presentation because of the strongly pro-Satan tendency of much recent criticism of *Paradise Lost*.

Usually when a critic dislikes an author, he doesn't go to the trouble of writing a book to say so, but Milton has inspired an unusual amount of unfavourable as well as favourable criticism, especially in this century. Paradoxically, the hostile critics can often stimulate a new reader of Milton more than those who praise him for the conventional reasons. From the beginning, his strong person-ality and decided political and religious opinions have made it difficult to hold him at a distance.

The *Critical Heritage* volume (ed. J. SHAWCROSS, Routledge, 1970), which contains virtually everything written by the first generation of critics, shows that political feeling was the chief obstacle to his appreciation in the late seventeenth and early eighteenth century. J. THORPE, *Milton Criticism, Selections from Four Centuries* (Routledge, 1961; paperback, 1965) gives a good picture of the way in which attitudes to Milton have altered between ADDISON's *Spectator* papers on *Paradise Lost* (1712) and the 1940s. Among the most interesting studies included are JONATHAN RICHARDSON's remarks on Milton's style, still fresh and perceptive though written in 1734, and part of SAMUEL JOHNSON's splendid essay, both sensible and cranky, from his *Lives of the Poets* (1779). Shorter extracts in both verse and prose include BLAKE's famous declaration in *The Marriage of Heaven and Hell* (1793) that Milton was 'a true Poet and of the Devil's party without knowing it'.

The most interesting Miltonic controversy of the eighteenth century was sparked off by the publication in 1732 of an edition of *Paradise Lost* by RICHARD BENTLEY. On the convenient hypothesis that whoever took down the poem at Milton's dictation had been either stupid or hard of hearing, Bentley freely altered any words or phrases inconsistent with his idea of Milton. Other critics stepped in to defend the original text and the resulting debate—as WILLIAM EMPSON notes in 'Milton and Bentley' (from *Some Versions of Pastoral*, Chatto, 1935; Peregrine, 1966)—showed that Bentley had been right in thinking some of his examples odd and ambiguous, though wrong in assuming that Milton had not wanted them to be so. Readers who can't get hold of Bentley's rare edition should look at the Empson essay, as also at *Milton's Grand Style* (Oxford U.P., 1963, paperback 1967) by CHRISTOPHER RICKS, who finds in the eighteenth-century critics many examples of the kind of close, intelligent reading which he then goes on to develop himself.

The nineteenth-century's admiration for Milton was based more on the 'feel' of his work than on a close scrutiny of it. SHELLEY, as an avowed atheist, could say that Milton's Satan was morally superior to his God, but most writers avoided a direct collision with the theology of *Paradise Lost* by ignoring the subject altogether. This may be one reason why there was a revival of interest in other works of his; the sonnets, in particular, were much imitated. The publication of his newly discovered *Christian Doctrine* in 1825 shocked many readers who had been regarding *Paradise Lost* as second only to the Bible in sacred authority, though it also made scholars aware that Puritanism was a more complex phenomenon than was generally realized. By the end of the century, Milton's political, scientific and religious views had ceased to be part of man's common experience, and one feels that critics were afraid to look too closely at his works, especially *Paradise Lost*, in case they might not like what they found. The time was ripe for an attack on the supposedly divine, perfect, and uncriticizable poet.

The attack took two forms: dislike of his style and its influence on literature, and dislike of his subject matter and attitudes. It was accompanied by a rediscovery of the seventeenth-century tradition of metaphysical, satiric, and erotic literature; poets found that they could learn from this as they could not from Milton. T. S. ELIOT, in 1936, took up Keats's complaint that *Paradise Lost* had killed the English blank verse epic, although in a 1947 lecture (reprinted with the earlier one in a Faber paperback, 1968) he gave Milton his qualified approval and decided that young poets might have something to learn from him after all. F. R. LEAVIS, who has also criticized Milton's style pretty severely, nevertheless admits to having carried and consistently read Milton throughout the 1914–18 War, and maintains that his and Eliot's qualified admiration is of greater value to Milton studies than the obfuscation of many scholars.

Two valuable defences of *Paradise Lost* from an orthodox point of view are CHARLES WILLIAMS's 1940 introduction to the World's Classics edition of Milton (reprinted in Thorpe) and C. S. LEWIS's *Preface to Paradise Lost*. Lewis went so far in combatting the 'romantic' view of Satan, however, as to disturb many readers who had not previously thought themselves given to devil-worship. Most people who come fresh to the poem find Satan the most exciting thing in it, and to tell them, as Lewis did, that he is really only a comic and egotistical failure is to destroy much of its interest for them. A. J. A. WALDOCK's *Paradise Lost and Its Critics* (Cambridge U.P., 1947; paperback, 1961) is basically a reply to Lewis, taking an enthusiastic pro-Satan and anti-God view which is very enjoyable to read, though it frequently misrepresents Milton. Reading him and Lewis together is an excellent introduction to the difficulties of interpreting *Paradise Lost*.

Waldock assumed that the reader's instinctive preference of Satan to God was the result of a failure on Milton's part. WILLIAM EMPSON, on the other hand, thinks that the poem succeeds precisely because of its moral confusions. *Milton's God* (Chatto, 1965) rewrites the epic from Satan's point of view and is often just plain wrong, but some of his comments ('I think it [*Paradise Lost*] horrible and wonderful . . . like Aztec or Benin sculpture or . . . the novels of Kafka') stimulate the imagination more than the work of more balanced and accurate critics.

The same might be said of ROBERT GRAVES's brilliantly unfair novel, *Wife to Mr Milton* (Cassell, 1944), which recreates the atmosphere of the early seventeenth century from the point of view of Milton's first wife. Though Mr Graves carries his dislike of Milton to the point of accepting an old Royalist slander that Milton deliberately inserted a prayer from the *Arcadia* into *Eikon Basilike* in order to use it against the king, his stiff, disagreeable poet is nevertheless the most interesting character in the book. Milton, we know, loved an argument. Perhaps that is why his reputation seems to thrive under attack.

It is thanks to the many anti-Milton writings earlier this century that so much excellent criticism has been appearing in the last two decades. Two of the most balanced and sympathetic studies, by writers who do not find admiration for Milton and the metaphysicals mutually exclusive, are J. H. SUMMERS, *The Muse's Method* (Chatto, 1962) and HELEN GARDNER, *A Reading of Paradise Lost* (Oxford U.P., 1965). I. G. MACCAFFREY, *Paradise Lost as Myth* (Harvard U.P., 1959) and NORTHROP FRYE, *Five Essays on Milton's Epics* (Routledge, 1966) are particularly interesting for the way in which (despite their titles) they treat not only Milton's epics but his other works as well in relation to archetypal patterns of human experience. PATRICK MURRAY, *Milton in the Twentieth Century* (Longmans 1967) is a useful survey of the work of twentieth century critics and scholars.

Finally, a few anthologies of good critical essays written in this century: *The Living Milton* (ed. F. KERMODE, Routledge, 1960), *The Lyric and Dramatic Milton* (ed. J. H. SUMMERS, Columbia U.P., 1965), *Milton's Epic Poetry* (ed. C. A. PATRIDES, Peregrine, 1967), and *Approaches to Paradise Lost* (ed. C. A. PATRIDES, Edward Arnold, 1968).

Places to visit

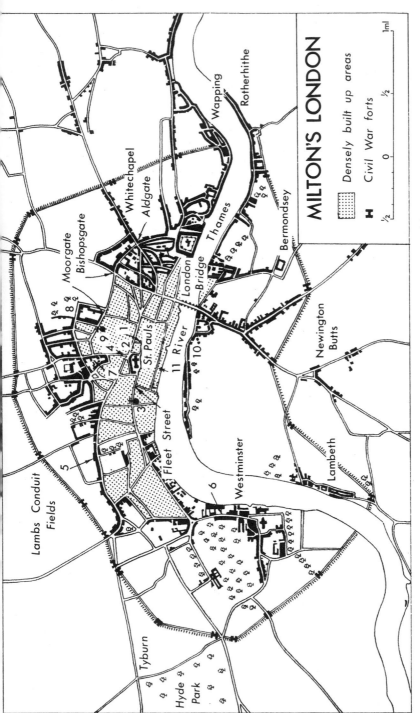

MILTON'S LONDON

::::: Densely built up areas

⊢⊣ Civil War forts

½   0   ½   1ml

Wapping

Rotherhithe

Whitechapel
Aldgate

Moorgate
Bishopsgate

Bermondsey

Thames

London
Bridge

St. Pauls

11 River

Newington
Butts

Fleet Street

Lambeth

Westminster

Lambs Conduit
Fields

Tyburn

Hyde
Park

1 Bread Street, Milton's birthplace. Destroyed in Great Fire of 1666
2 St. Paul's School, the nearest grammar school to his home
3 St. Bride's Churchyard, Milton's home on returning from his continental travels
4 Aldersgate Street where Milton took his first wife and wrote his early pamphlets
5 High Holborn where Milton resided briefly in 1648–9 and 1663
6 Whitehall, where Milton occupied official apartments in Scotland Yard and Petty France. His first and second wives died here
7 Bartholomew Close, Milton's secret residence after the Restoration

10. Globe Theatre, Shakespeare's company's summer amphitheatre
11. Blackfriars Theatre, the company's indoor winter hall. In 1645 he moved to nearby Barbican

8. Bunhill Fields, Milton's last home occupied after his third marriage in 1663

One cannot very well make a Milton pilgrimage. The heart of the 'Shakespeare country' is a small village with no other claim to importance, but 'Milton country' is London, which has changed out of all recognition since his time. None of his many London houses is still standing: the Great Fire of 1666 and the Second World War between them took care of almost everything he knew except a few churches, Westminster Abbey, and part of Whitehall (see map). Still, it is possible to visit St Giles, Cripplegate, on weekday mornings. The church is now embedded in multistorey office blocks and flats on the Barbican site, but it contains a monument (erected 1793) commemorating Milton's burial there; the original grave-stone disappeared only five years after his death, when the chancel floor was raised. From St Giles, it is a short walk to Bartholomew Close, where Milton lived in hiding after the Restoration. The little streets keep their old shape, though not their old houses, and give some idea of the London he would have known.

As one would expect, Westminster Abbey has a monument to Milton (erected about 1738) in its Poets' Corner. The National Portrait Gallery is an obvious place to go in search of Miltonic atmosphere; the poet's portrait as a Cambridge student is surrounded by those of other seventeenth-century writers and thinkers, and nearby is a whole roomful of serious-looking generals and fighters on both sides of the Civil War.

It is easier to find Milton outside London. The cottage at Chalfont

Christ's College, Cambridge, from D. Loggan's *Cantabrigia Illustrata, 1688*

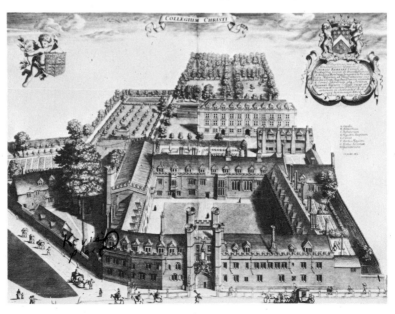

St Giles, where he stayed briefly in 1665, is now a Milton museum (illustrated on p. 33). The ruins of Ludlow Castle, Shropshire, where *Comus* was first acted, are open to the public. The masque itself is sometimes performed close by. The Bodleian Library at Oxford has a few Milton relics, but Trinity College, Cambridge, is really the place to visit: its magnificent library has a manuscript in Milton's own handwriting (see p. 116), which contains corrected drafts of many of the early poems, including *Comus* and *Lycidas*. Half a mile down the street from Trinity is Christ's College, much of which still looks as it did in the seventeenth century. There is a room which is said, with no real evidence, to have been his (Wordsworth got drunk in it one night); just outside is 'Milton's Walk'; and in one of the courts there is a mulberry tree which he almost certainly did *not* plant, though of course there is a tradition that he did.

General Index

Works, apart from anonymous ones, appear under the name of their author. For works by Milton, see separate index, page 189.

Index to Milton's Works